Julie and Bob,
Success can happen if we
never give up!

♡, Meredith B. Kessler
Aaron Kessler

Life of a Triathlete
Race Preparation

Authors: Meredith B. Kessler & Aaron Kessler

Editor: Kate Bolen
Copyeditor: Claire Kessler
Photographer (cover): Sue Hutter
Foreword: Christopher Wright

Success can happen if we
never give up!

Contents

"Remembering that you are going to die is the best way I know to avoid the trap of thinking you have something to lose. You are already naked. There is no reason not to follow your heart." —Steve Jobs' Stanford Commencement Address

FOREWORD

It happens during every Ironman, to almost every athlete. Everyone, from the gifted professional to the serious age-grouper to those hoping only to finish, has a dark period when distance and depletion lead to despair. Those bad patches are all but unavoidable, and it is how we deal with them that ultimately determines success or failure on the day. It is through the crucible of this test that every participant, fast or slow, woman or man, rich or poor, must pass.

Most recently, I experienced this at Ironman Coeur d'Alene, where after a decent day to that point, the wheels were beginning to come off around mile nine of the run. All that pre-race confidence and bravado was evaporating rapidly in the face of the harsh realities of the day. My pace was unraveling as quickly as my mental equanimity, and the future looked bleak.

Out of nowhere, I felt a reassuring hand on my shoulder. "Looking strong, Chris," murmured a familiar voice. With what little energy remained, I turned my head in disbelief to see the runner next to me. It will hopefully go some way toward conveying her unparalleled generosity of spirit that even when she was leading an Ironman, Meredith Kessler would take precious time and energy to offer a kind word of encouragement. "Keep it steady," she smiled, "and you'll be fine."

As Meredith moved confidently on, smoothly ticking off miles at the relentless pace that demolished her competitors and took her to yet another victory that day, I watched her go in astonishment. This was a two-loop run, of course, and I was a good hour-and-a-half behind her…but here was the day's champion, selflessly sharing her energy, even before she was done. It was all but impossible not to soak up some of that calm, effective resolve, and I quickly transitioned from wallowing in how awful I felt to generating solutions. Calories, caffeine, and Meredith's favorite mantra (Keep Calm and Carry On) solved the problem, and I had a strong final third of the run to finish in a new personal record. The saying that one kind word can make a world of difference is a hackneyed and overused cliché. It also happened on this particular day to be true.

The ego and vanity and excess that drench other professional sports seem, sadly, to be seeping slowly into triathlon. Our sport is fortunate to have Meredith Kessler as a bulwark against that outcome. Her message is one of kindness and moderation, of common sense and life balance. Would that we all listen, and let us hope that this book helps us to do just that.

I feel extraordinarily fortunate to have become a friend of this utterly remarkable individual. Of course, she is not Superwoman—she cannot personally encourage and teach every athlete on the course. Or can she? The more I thought about it, the more I inclined to the view that this book constitutes, for all who are lucky enough to read it, Meredith's reassuring hand on *their* shoulders. The words it contains are her quiet wisdom, unselfishly made available to anyone who wants to become the best triathlete and the best human being they can possibly be. That is a path along which Meredith Kessler has progressed further than just about anyone else I know.

Christopher Wright
September 1st, 2012
Los Angeles

INTRODUCTION: HOW TO USE THE BOOK

In an ideal world, becoming a pro triathlete meant that I would wake up, work out, get massages, have a dietician plan my meals, and still have time for family and friends. In reality, this was far from the truth. The nature of my work changed from my days spent in my career at the investment bank RBC Capital Markets. Nevertheless, I still could not find enough hours in the day to accomplish everything I set out to do. The stakes of the races became higher because it was now my sole source of income and livelihood. No longer could I count on that steady paycheck from my banking job.

From the very beginning of this triathlon journey, I have felt extremely lucky and privileged to be able to support myself as an athlete. Yet I could never have foreseen the trials and tribulations that came with being a professional triathlete. My working hours are divided between a number of activities, not the least of which still finds me in front of a computer most of the day, struggling to fit in my training schedule just as I did at my banking job. The difference is that I am working at home. However, I truly am thankful every day that I get to do what I love. I also contemplate what my life would have been like these past several years as an amateur and pro if I could have had a guide laying the foundation—someone who could have taught me how to prepare myself to race each race in optimal condition.

The best way to begin this book is to relay to you what it is *not*. This is *not* a self-help guide promoting ways to increase your mental toughness to succeed in the triathlon world. This is *not* a rah-rah book where I share my life lessons and try to give you hope that reaching your goals in the tri world is possible. This is *not* a self-congratulatory book where I go through my race accomplishments and inform the reader how I overcame many obstacles, showing my grit and determination. This is *not* a workout book where I spell out endless pages of my routines and say how this plan will allow everyone to achieve greatness. This is *not* a book where I will give you mantras or sayings that will propel you to greatness during a race. We have all read these kinds of books in one form or another, and the value is limited to the desperation of the reader.

This is not your typical triathlete guidebook where I take you through detailed workouts, what gear I use and why, and how to use this gear. I figure if you are reading this book, you already have your routine down, or you have someone in your life that you are working with who provides this information. It took me years of training with other triathletes plus hiring my former coach, Matt Dixon, to learn all the intricacies of the sport, and the learning never stops. Writing a book about these concepts would be futile since it is constantly evolving and often boils down to personal preference.

This *is* a practical guide to laying the foundation for success as a pro athlete in the triathlon world. There are tips, techniques, and real-life stories that will help triathletes of any ability, even though it is written for the niche audience of top amateur and pro triathletes. Thinking like and emulating a pro will only improve your overall performance.

The past fifteen years have been spent learning everything I could through discussions with coaches, advisors, fellow triathletes, and some of the top nutritionists in the country. I am not a doctor, nor do I have a degree in physical education, but I have raced over fifty Ironmans, learning something new from each one. I do not think you should have to race over fifty Ironmans to learn what I know. My desire is to greatly shorten that learning curve.

The *Life of a Triathlete* series will fill the informational void in the triathlete world by giving specific direction to those wishing to embark on this exciting journey. The overall objective is to reduce the ramp time it takes individuals to go from beginner to amateur, amateur to top amateur, or top amateur to pro, so they can spend their time competing and not being tripped up by the "little" things that plague every athlete's entry into the sport. This is a culmination of over a decade of experiences, races, successes, and failures, and it will continue to be a learning experience. Yes, there are tremendous publications out there that serious triathletes should be reading, such as *Triathlete Magazine* and *Lava Magazine*, though the information is scattered and often just relevant to "hot topics" of the month. What I have created is a series of instructional guides you can reference at any time, where all the information you need to help you succeed is collected in one place.

Being a pro in any sport is a lot like being a cook. It starts off as your passion, and you soak up knowledge like a sponge in order to be better at your craft. The cook then becomes the head of the kitchen, and eventually the owner of a restaurant, and a lot of extracurricular noise begins to interrupt the purity of cooking. There are now bills, employees, patrons to please, and you are pushed in a number of directions, all of them opposite of your true passion of cooking. Triathletes are no different as they take the steps from beginners, to amateurs, to strong amateurs, and to pros. The keys are to not lose sight of why you love the profession and to develop creative ways to stay motivated.

The reason this analogy is important is it brought me to my current state: I never wanted to lose the passion for my sport, yet it is now my business and I have to think of it as my career. I enjoy helping others, however, there are not enough hours in the day to advise everyone in the tri community without taking away from my personal and professional objectives. There are definitely mediums and forums where people can find information; still nothing beats the know-how of someone who has experienced a multitude of challenging situations firsthand. I decided to switch my business from a technician-based entity (one that is dependent on my physical work) and transition it to an entrepreneur-based business. By doing this, I can provide content to the triathlon community while continuing on my professional journey with less clutter in my life. The use of technology will enable me to reach a larger audience and to have more of an impact in a tri community that craves information on the sport.

The world of triathlon is growing at an enormous pace, and the *Life of a Triathlete* series is a tremendous medium to help others. I am amazed by the constant outpouring of questions—brief inquires through social media, perceptive questions from the growing crowds at pro panels, and curious advice seeking from my fellow triathletes in the San Francisco community, as we all strive to improve. I am in a unique position to answer the questions of a large segment of this population, and I do not take it lightly. I know the uncomfortable feeling of not knowing what to do in the transitions, how many calories to ingest on the bike, or how much it will cost to get to a race and compete.

In my early days as an amateur, and when I turned pro, I was very lucky to have a few friends who took me under their wings and gave me thoughtful advice. Even with this bit of luck, though, I found the learning process was painful and unforgiving. My husband and I have purposely not read many of the tri books in the marketplace because we wanted our book to have a fresh perspective on the sport. We have catalogued countless questions (I probably receive ten emails per week asking questions concerning different aspects of the life of a triathlete), and we hope to cover the majority by providing answers through my experiences.

The idea to write *Life of a Triathlete* came to me after an accomplished pro of six years approached me and asked, "How do I get a bike sponsor? Can you help me?" I then realized that the road each professional triathlete follows has the same twists, turns, and detours that I have faced. Questions relating to a bike sponsor or hiring an agent are a few of the many stumbling blocks we all run into. So, here I was, a young pro, answering the question for the experienced pro, and thus, my thoughts turned to figuring out a way to get this information out to everyone.

Amateurs look to emulate pro athletes in their pursuit of their goals, so it made sense to start at the top of the pyramid—to first dissect the life of a pro triathlete and then examine my journey from top amateur to pro. The skills and techniques learned in these first two volumes will translate not only to amateur athletes but also to individuals searching for organization in their everyday lives. It is safe to say that how I approach being a pro triathlete, running my business, and living my personal life is still a work in progress. I feel strongly, though, that it *can be done*, and these are the ideas I want to share with my readers.

The term "expert" is tossed around freely these days. I imagine that I am in the top 0.00001 percent of the people in the world as far as number of Ironmans and Triathlons I have *completed*, so I will make the assumption that this qualifies me as an expert. My book dissects the life I lead as a pro triathlete and what has helped or hindered my path to becoming an Ironman champion, being a consistent podium finisher (finishing in first through fifth place), and acquiring an income that allows me to continue to pursue my dreams. As I mentioned before, the topic is about the niche pro world; however, through this amateurs can learn how an elite athlete approaches her profession.

These manuals are by no means the Holy Grail of triathlon—far from it. This is the story of what works for me, which may not translate for everyone. However, the ideas and concepts expressed can be the foundation for how you approach your sport, and many aspects can be used to fit into the puzzle that is your life. I suggest you take a look at the chapters, bounce around to ones you feel are relevant to your interests right now, and come back on a consistent basis to continue to grow your triathlon knowledge as new situations arise. There are some chapters, like "Taxes," which may not be relevant at this time but could be later on as you begin your own business.

As you will learn, the sport is not big enough at this time to be able to afford agents, lawyers, estate planners, etc., so it is imperative you think outside the box and learn things on your own in order to grow your passion into a business. It is a true start-up venture to take the path from amateur athlete to elite pro, but it is one that is not impossible. I hope to give you guidance along the way through this series, and I will continue to add content as the playing field changes and new circumstances unfold.

My husband and I individually contribute to each chapter based on our personal experiences. Hopefully the use of "our," "we," "I," and "me" will not be too confusing. We felt it was appropriate to tell our story in this manner since we have taken this journey together. I have the perspective of someone who has learned triathlon through trial and error over many years, while simultaneously developing my business skills as a manager at the Ritz Carlton, Club One, and RBC Capital Markets. My husband has been by my side throughout, watching me develop from a struggling amateur to a pro. During the time, he also helped me maintain my triathlon business while he successfully managed his career in finance. He had a very successful baseball career at Harvard University, and played football, baseball, and basketball in high school, so he has a keen eye for what to do and not to do to achieve goals in both business and athletics. This combination of a stable business partnership and creative thinking in managing our lives has led us to a unique perspective on navigating this hectic world while maintaining balance in career and overall life activities.

I have high hopes that people who read this book will take something away that will help them become better triathletes, game-day racers, organizers, and businesspeople. When I graduated from college, I never thought I would be authoring a book about the triathlon world, but life has a funny way of changing its course to present new avenues and challenges. So it is with great pleasure I present *Life of a Triathlete: Race Preparation* and *Life of a Triathlete: Business*, the first volumes in a series of manuals designed to help triathletes begin and maintain their journey through the exciting sport of triathlon.

PREFACE

It was the second race in a row where I failed to understand a piece of information that ultimately led to a catastrophic event. Once again I fell short of my goal of finishing my fortieth Ironman. I came to the realization that athletes are conquered in a triathlon more often by what they do not know than by their physical or mental shortcomings. Pro triathletes, in general, reach their peak at age thirty and continue to excel into their mid thirties. What happened to their twenties and the prime age span for athletes in every other sport? Why is Lebron James peaking through his late twenties and Chrissie Wellington not reaching her potential until she is past thirty? The key, I believe, is experience and the lack of specific knowledge of my sport even though, at the age of thirty-two, I was a seasoned pro in my fortieth Ironman. Lebron James will be on the downside of his career at this age while I am still learning and peaking. Why is this?

My husband pulled me out of Ironman Coeur d'Alene because there was clearly something wrong. I probably would not have stopped on my own until I passed out, like my previous race at Ironman St. George. I had completed thirty-nine Ironmans and could not finish my fortieth and I had to remind myself that I was lucky to get to this point without any major setbacks. The enormous list of elements that needs to come together in order for a pro triathlete to achieve success on a particular day is astronomical; consequently, adversity comes with the territory of pro competition. This factor led me to the creation of the first books in a series of triathlon books, *Life of a Triathlete: Race Preparation* and *Life of a Triathlete: Business*. I want to use my triathlon experiences to help better prepare both up and coming and prospective pro triathletes to deal with the peaks and valleys of an unforgiving sport.

No one knows what they are doing when they start out in triathlon, and the learning curve takes time, money, determination, and effort. It took me over twenty Ironman races to realize that I was floundering in the sport. This prompted me to enlist the help of my former coach, Matt Dixon, founder and head coach of *purplepatch*. A coach is a step in the right direction, although it is only one of the many pieces of the puzzle that will help you achieve your goals in the grueling tri sport.

It seems ludicrous to me now I had no idea that I needed multiple electrolyte tabs in the dry heat of St. George. As I left the bike to run transition, I did not know I was a "dead man walking" because I was not properly prepared for the marathon "death march" in ninety degree heat. My body had somehow limped through other extremely hot races (participating as an amateur in Kona comes to mind), however, I was not competing at the level in those previous races that I was as a pro at St. George. Needless to say, I made it to the twenty-second mile and passed out, all alone in second place. The $3,000 hospital bill and loss of podium and sponsorship dollars was an expensive lesson to learn. This was an estimated $20,000-$25,000 hit from potential earnings and paid expenses because of my lack of nutritional knowledge comprehension of how my body was reacting in the heat.

Mackenzie Lobby wrote the following in the June 2012 issue of *Triathlete Magazine* in her article "Better With Age": "Despite the fact that age brings a loss in muscle mass, bone density, and maximal aerobic capacity, it also brings experience, which may play a greater role in triathlon than in other sports. Consider the fact that triathletes generally don't pick up the sport until later in life, and that triathletes need to master not one discipline, but three." She goes on to say that track athletes reach their peak at age twenty-six and swimmers at age twenty-one.

Lebron James has been perfecting his craft of playing basketball since he was old enough to hold a round ball. Sidney Crosby was skating before he could walk and had been playing organized hockey for twelve years before he became a professional. I did not ride a bike until after college and had no clue what an Ironman was until I was twenty-three. Triathletes do not have the support system in place that other sports do, so athlete's learning curves happen in their twenties which is most likely why they peak in their early thirties. There are no mentors or instructional manuals on how to succeed in the sport. Many individuals have tried to write books, but they all focus on training. The focus in this series will be on *everything but training*, which is where I believe the majority of race day failures reside.

In the *Triathlete Magazine* article, Mackenzie Lobby goes on to say, "For younger athletes looking to reach that peak sooner rather than later, author Malcolm Gladwell's '10,000-hour rule' may apply. It states that one must engage in an activity for at least 10,000 hours before they are mastering that specific task." I would argue that, without the proper guidance, triathletes spend many, many hours struggling to figure out this sport, and the possibility of blowing through the "10,000 hour rule" is real. It is imperative to not let this happen, or the athlete's ability to lead a normal, healthy life interacting with friends and family will suffer.

My goal with this triathlon series is to cut the embedded learning curve by three to five years. The effects of cutting the time it takes for athletes to realize their potential would have a ground-breaking impact on the sport of triathlon. Pro athletes would be at their peak longer to create a stronger connection with the fans; amateur athletes would not get discouraged as quickly, and stay with the sport longer; there would be fewer injuries and a larger pool of individuals, creating better competition.

This is not to say that I have not learned from my setbacks and misfortunes-quite the contrary. The heart-wrenching failure that all triathletes feel at some time in their careers continues to motivate them to eventually overcome the obstacles. There is no other sport that pushes the individual to such highs and lows, and there is no way to completely avoid this journey. However, this sport has a variety of challenges. If I can help people avoid some of the pitfalls so they can reach their goals faster, I have done my job. Yes, it will always be an uphill battle, but hopefully my story will guide athletes towards efficiently picking and choosing which battle to fight.

I can only dream of what my amateur- and pro-athletic career would have been like if I had this manual before I began my journey. The overlooked details that caused countless setbacks would have been avoided, placing me further along my athletic path. If I would have known to closely follow the weather for St. George and had taken into account that my body requires more than the average person's water and electrolyte intake, I would not have passed out on the twenty-second mile and sacrificed $20,000 in revenue. My intent is to provide information, other than training, for the triathlete to be in the best position to meet their goals and succeed.

I received the message below from a concerned fan and race volunteer a few days after Ironman St. George 2011. Although I appreciate the genuine concern, I am determined to never receive another similar email again. My objective with this book is to help athletes avoid this same scenario and learn from the experience of a pro triathlete.

> Name: Cheryl
> Company: St George IM
> Message: I don't think you will remember the last few minutes before you passed out Saturday. I was the one who walked beside you for a few minutes until you sat down, laid back and passed out. I hope you are back to health now!

Life of a Triathlete: Race Preparation
Life of a Triathlete: Business

ATHLETE PROFILE

Information as of February 1st, 2016

Name: Meredith Kessler
City: San Francisco/Marin County
Profession: Pro Triathlete, Triathlon Coach, Cycling Instructor, Writer
Height: 5 feet 8 inches
Weight: 130 pounds
Shoe size: 8.5 (United States sizing)
Bike shoe size: 39 (European sizing)
Body fat: 14 percent
Sweat test fluid loss rate: 17.32 milliliters per minute
Focus: Full Ironman and 70.3 distances
Secondary focus: 10K, Half Marathon, ITU, Olympic Triathlon distances

Apparel: Saucony
Bike: Ventum One
Bike size: 54 centimeters
Bike chain: 54
Bike chainwheel: 55T and 42T flat courses; 53T and 39T hilly courses
Bike seat: ISM
Cassette: 11/23 flat courses; 11/28 hilly courses
Cycling gear: ROKA Sports
Components: Shimano Di2 – 11 speed
Components bottom bracket, pulley wheels, wheel bearings, chain: Ceramic Speed
Component lubricant and treatment: Atomic High Performance
Crank size: 165 millimeters
Electrolytes: BASE Performance Electrolyte Salt
Energy: Red Bull
Granola: Bungalow Munch
Goggles: ROKA Sports
Helmet: Rudy Project

Kit: Saucony
Listening device (training sessions): yurbuds
Nutrition: Gels and blocks (variety of brands)
Power meter: PowerTap
Shoes: Saucony Kinvara
Sunglasses: Rudy Project
Tires: Challenge – Record 24 millimeters
Wearable technology: Lumo Run
Wetsuit: ROKA Sports
Wheels: Enve Composites

Recovery: Recovery Boots
Recovery: Vector450
Weight training: Kate Ligler, personal trainer
Outdoor training temperature: Average 65 degrees
Outside cycling per week: 9 hours
Inside cycling per week: 8 hours
Outside running per week: 3 sessions
Inside treadmill running per week: 3 sessions
Free water swimming per week: 0 yards
Pool swimming per week: 30,000 – 55,000 yards
Weight training per week: 2 sessions
Other training: Occasional trail running and Bikram yoga
Total hours training per week: 25–30 hours
Massages: Average one session every two-three weeks; more as age has increased

Sponsors/Partners: Atomic High Performance, Bungalow Munch, Ceramic Speed, Challenge Tires, Eminess Design, Enve Composites, Holony Media, ISM, Kit Order, Lumo Run, Play2Health, PowerTap, Recovery Pump, Red Bull, ROKA Sports, Rudy Project, Saucony, Shimano, TriBike Transport, ShiftSF, Vector 450, Ventum Cycling, XLAB Aerodynamic Hydration, ZÜPA Noma

Twitter handle: @mbkessler
Instagram username: @mbkessler
Website: www.meredithkessler.com
Website: www.lifeoftriathlete.com

Facebook: www.facebook.com/meredith.b.kessler
Facebook fan page: www.facebook.com/mbkessler55
LinkedIn: www.linkedin.com/in/meredithkessler55
YouTube: www.youtube.com/user/MeredithKessler55

OFF-SEASON—PREPARING FOR THE YEAR

I designed this book to tell the story of how I approach each year, starting with the North American off-season, which is usually between November and March, depending on an athlete's schedule. Unfortunately the "off-season" for a pro begins around August. Even then, we are reaching out to sponsors, trying to secure sponsorship for the following year before the Ironman World Championship in Kona.

I have seen a lot of approaches to fitness in the off-season, and each one has its benefits and drawbacks. There is a school of thought that this is the time to let your body go and to live a little before the training starts up again full bore in February. There are also those who stay fit but go into full recovery mode to heal all of the nagging injuries that plagued them throughout the season. These are both fine strategies if you have the discipline to be able to pick back up where you left off the previous year. However, at races at the beginning of the season I hear athletes lamenting they do not have their running legs yet or that they are building for the rest of the year.

I treat my training in the season and off-season as one continuous process—a life-style that should not be disrupted and a discipline that should always be improving, not bouncing around like a yo-yo. If there is balance in my life during the season with family, friends, business, and enjoying a glass of wine, then there should be no need to do anything differently in the off-season. Lebron James is not letting himself go in the off-season only to try to rush back into shape during the preseason. His workout routine allows him to keep improving his craft, and he will come into the first game of the next year an improved player. Instead of needing a month or two to get into game shape, he will be at the top of his game right away, because he continued his training and learned new moves and techniques to keep him among the elite NBA basketball players.

Working out is something I have been doing my whole life, and it would be foreign to me to incorporate tapering or extended periods of down time. The objective is to strive to improve, whether it is in fitness, nutrition, hydration, or a deficiency you recognize in your overall tri regimen. This is delayed if the off-season is treated as a long vacation. If you do not treat the year as one big event, your peaks and valleys will feel like pedaling uphill to catch up to where you were the year before. What you want is nice steady improvement of your overall fitness, even in the off-season, to keep pushing that peak to greater heights.

The off-season provides the triathlete's chance to absorb information and practice different techniques to incorporate into races in the upcoming year. If you attempt a crash course a week before your race, you will inevitably fail to reach your goals because you are not prepared. You should strive to become a meticulous triathlete, coming into every situation prepared and not being distracted when adversity is thrown your way. You want to strive to be a consistent finisher who steadily improves, rather than the athlete who strings together a few good races and a few not so good races.

Race Schedule

One of the first objectives for a pro during the off-season is to figure out a race schedule. Sponsors require you give them your races as soon as possible so they can target their contracts accordingly. Since I do not actually have an off-season, I do not shy away from targeting races early in the triathlon race year. There are races around the globe as early as January, so you can always find something to suit your needs.

Races come in all shapes and sizes, and you do not have to compete in a triathlon to help maintain your fitness or improve a particular aspect of your race. I sprinkle in small swims, trail runs, or sprint bike races to work on my speed in these three events. In addition to the well-known Ironman, Revolution3 (REV3), 5150, Challenge, and HITS Triathlon Series races, there are hundreds of other triathlons across the globe. Utilize the Internet to find races that fit your schedule, and jump into these events. Do not forget to plan around important dates on your calendar, which might include your wedding, friends' weddings, bachelor or bachelorette parties, vacations, concerts, and family gatherings. Although you are triathlon racing, if you are serious about becoming a pro, it is important to keep your sanity by not omitting your life and the fun that comes with it.

Often there is some sort of racing fee associated with entering these events whether you are a pro or amateur. There could also be strict rules concerning entering these races if they sell out quickly, which means you have to target your event and make the decision well in advance of the actual date. In USA Triathlon racing, pro athletes do have a distinct advantage of dropping into a race a few weeks in advance of the event for an annual fee. For more information, go to www.usatriathlon.org to read about the rules for obtaining pro membership, the fee, and the regulations. Be aware, although you can drop into races throughout the year, you do have to give the race organizers ample time (two weeks) to prepare for your arrival. I have heard of pro athletes getting turned down because they only gave a week's notice. Remember, pros have to renew their pro card every year, and if they don't, they are not eligible for prize money and cannot race in the pro category.

As you pick your races, write down the contact information for the race directors and individuals associated with the event. You usually have to register online or via phone. If you are a pro, email them to introduce yourself and let them know you will be competing in their event next year. Ask them if there is anything you can do for exposure for the race, if they have deals for lodging or rental cars, or if they provide a stipend for pro racers. It cannot hurt to reach out to race organizers; they may recognize you down the road and remember how you graciously introduced yourself a few years back. Worst-case scenario is they thank you for reaching out and let you know they will be in touch. Best-case scenario is they have the bandwidth to be able to help you in some capacity.

As I mentioned, as a pro, you do have the luxury of being able to pick and choose your races throughout the year. However, this should not stop you from having a plan going into the season for your sponsors, training, and qualifying for the 70.3 World Championship, the

Revolution3 Championship, the ITU World Championship, or the Ironman World Championship. Whatever your objective, you need to know the rules about qualifying for each of these events, or you may be caught in July and August flying around the world to get yourself in the game. This does not bode well for the legs of a racer. One of the pluses of racing from October through December is some of the races may qualify you for the next year's tally, thus you can get a head start on your goal by knowing the rules for the series you are choosing.

In 2011, I had goals of qualifying as a pro for the Ironman Championship in Kona, so I raced Ironman Arizona in 2010, which counted as points for 2011. I then entered one of the first races of 2011 in the United States, the Ironman Texas 70.3, and received more points for Kona by finishing eighth. In my next two races at Ironman St. George and Ironman Coeur d'Alene, I took a detour and DNFed (did not finish), which left me out of contention for Kona. I then had to make the decision to shoot for Kona or just race and see what happened, so I chose the latter and entered REV3 Portland and finished first place. After much searching, I had determined what was wrong with my body and decided to race as much as possible the rest of the season, even though the goal of Kona was tantalizingly just out of my reach. This included a third place finish at Ironman Canada, second place at Ironman Wisconsin (this was in early September, so most individuals were already focused on Kona), and then third place at REV3 Anderson. I also qualified and jumped into the ITU Long Distance World Championships and finished third place for my final race, for point totals, of 2011. I then focused on 2012 and finished third at Ironman Arizona in November of 2011.

A triathlon season has so many twists and turns there is no way I could have foreseen any of it when I was piecing my year together in November of 2010. My initial goal of qualifying for Kona was shattered with two unfortunate races, but triathlon, like life, never ends up exactly how you planned it. My goal transitioned through the season from qualifying for Kona to figuring out why my body was breaking down during races to gaining experience and revenue by racing as much as possible. Even while writing portions of this manual in 2012, my season had thrown me for a loop because of an unexpected bike crash that forced me to alter the second half of my season at the time. The bottom line is, just like any good business, you have to adjust with what is thrown your way and change your expectations based on your ever-changing circumstances. Do not get discouraged, but be adaptable at what the sport throws at you; if it were easy, it would not be triathlon.

Period

This topic may only affect fifty percent of the population directly, but it applies to one hundred percent of it indirectly. Menstruation seems like an unusual topic to include in the off-season chapter, but if you are a woman, it does affect your entire season, and I might as well get it over with at the beginning of the book. When I figure out my race schedule at the end of the year for the following season, I create an Excel spreadsheet with all the dates where my period should fall, twenty-eight days after the previous one. This changes over the course of the season as my body is affected by outside influences such as training, diet, and stress, but this provides a fairly accurate road map as to when my period will hit in every given month.

If at all possible, do not schedule races around your period; give at least a three-day window on each side of the event. As with any race schedule, nothing goes exactly according to plan, but you can try to set yourself up for success by starting out the season scheduling races under the best conditions. Male readers who have female friends or partners competing in triathlon need to understand if a race falls on this fateful day, your companion will not have her best race and will thus be a bear to deal with.

I have competed in countess triathlons, so it has been impossible for me to completely avoid racing while on my period. In the days leading up to the race before your period, you feel like a Ferrari with all five gears in sync; then the day of the race, everything changes and you feel like a four-speed 1987 Yugo with no reserves. When you are racing the day of or around your period, you do not have that extra gear. This is triathlon, specifically a half or full Ironman, and you need every ounce of your body to complete the race, try to podium, and achieve your goals. You are so far from your top form that all you can think about is trying to finish, somehow.

There have been a few races where I could not avoid the dreaded period, and I toed the line to lackluster results. This is not to say I would have been on the podium if I did not have my period, but my times and position do not fall in line with my other performances, which is an indication something was not right. Vineman always seems to have an agreement with my period to hit at the exact same time. In the race in 2010, I was a sitting duck as the period hit the night before. I finished the event in a disappointing seventh place, but I was pleased I was able to push through the discomfort. However, when your business and livelihood depend on results, your period is not a productive business partner.

Although it was a treat to be there, my experiences at Kona have been very forgettable, race-wise. There is nothing you can do to schedule around Kona because it is the Super Bowl of the Ironman series. The date is set in stone and unavoidable. You cannot skip Kona if you have your period and then race another event of equal importance a few weeks later. I went into Kona as an amateur in 2008 coming off three straight second-place finishes, and my period hit me the night before the race. The heat and humidity on a normal day in Kona is enough to deal with, but add your period and it is unbearable. I finished an uninspiring seventeenth, and I do not even remember running the marathon—not the Kona experience I was looking for. My first race there as a pro was in 2010, and once again, my period had no remorse and hit me two days before the event. This gave me a little time to recover, but, ultimately, the period reared its ugly head at the wrong time and prevailed. I finished in twenty-sixth place and, again, do not remember running the marathon.

Although I am not a doctor, a doctor who is a friend told me he could not believe I raced Kona during my period because of all my body's liquid loss. In addition to the normal perspiration you have during an event, you also lose bodily fluids through your period, so you have to be cognizant of the fact your body will be more dehydrated than normal. With all my racing experience, I have no solution for racing during your period and can only relay to you what I know. It should be planned for, and you should avoid racing at all costs. If you do find yourself racing around your period, hydrate, then drink more, and then hydrate more. You will find yourself very uncomfortable, and it will be a mental battle to complete the race. If anything, racing around your period will put another notch in your belt with the confidence and knowledge that you can do it and that it will not defeat you.

It is impossible to race at your peak condition every time; there will always be something that is annoying to the hyper vigilant, Type A triathlete. However, the goal is to put yourself in the best position to succeed. Part of this is using your off-season to look for courses that suit your style and have conditions to your liking, and part of it is being able to avoid the races that coincide with your period cycle. I know there are ways to alleviate your period, such as birth control pills, but this really put a spin on the inner workings of my body and was not for me. The pill created other problems for me that outweighed the two to three days of discomfort I feel with my period; I did not want to become a walking experiment by using pills to cure every ailment I was presented with. I also began omitting caffeine in 2012, which played a role in reducing the pain I experienced around and during my period. Caffeine dehydrates the body, and since I sweat more than most individuals, this was a natural omission from my diet.

On a side note, there have been tons of studies on the effects of caffeine during training and in races. I know a lot of pros who get through their workouts and racing with copious amounts of caffeine in one form or another, and it does help them. However, for my weak kidneys and problems with dehydration, caffeine does not work, even though I love the taste of coffee.

In summary, there are no 'cure alls' for racing with your period and, as I have mentioned, your best bet is to schedule races around your cycle. Of course, we are triathletes and often have to follow the races whenever they fall so just know you are not alone on this journey and the phrase 'this too shall pass' seems to work well here.

Resume

As a pro triathlete, you need a resume just like any other job applicant.

You should send your resume to sponsors, potential coaches, media outlets, and anyone to whom you want to introduce yourself. The resume should be professional looking and highlight significant amateur races and all pro races to show how you have improved. It is one thing to send an email to a race director or sponsor, but it is another to include a slick looking resume that contains all of your information in one easy to read synopsis of your career.

As I reach out to potential sponsors, I always include a cover letter explaining the benefits of a partnership and my goals for the upcoming season (see *Life of a Triathlete: Business* for details on this cover letter). I also include my resume in PDF format so my accomplishments are not listed unprofessionally in a haphazard email. When I flew to Interbike in Las Vegas, the grand show for everything cycling and triathlon, I met company representatives at the booths with my business card and my resume, just like an eager applicant at a job fair. As with any resume, I made sure there were no typos or misinformation, because those are the first ones that are thrown by the wayside, no matter how well I might have performed.

Your resume should be updated every six months with your race results, current racing pictures, and sponsor logos. I was fortunate to have pro triathlete friends, Linsey Corbin for example, who shared their resumes with me, and I was able to choose the best aspects as models for my profile. I have included my resume below to provide an example of how you could approach it and to give you a sense of what a resume should accomplish. Since space is limited in this book, I cannot include the colorful pictures, my logo, sponsor logos, and formatting that make my resume unique to me, however, be creative and make yours unique to you. This is a sample from my early years as a professional.

<Include your personal logo>
Meredith Kessler
www.meredithkessler.com
<phone number>

<racing photo>

Meredith grew up in Columbus, Ohio, where she was a four-sport athlete and was inducted into her high school's Athletic Hall of Fame. She went on to receive a Division I athletic scholarship at Syracuse University where she participated in field hockey and track.

After graduation in 2000, she used her graduation money to purchase her first bike and entered in a full Ironman two weeks later. From that moment on, she caught the spirit of Ironman competition and hasn't looked back. Since that first Ironman in 2000, Meredith has competed in 42 full Ironman races all over the United States and Canada.

She was undefeated in her 2009 season having been the 1st place amateur woman in every race that year. In addition, she holds the amateur course record at Ironman Arizona and the age-group course record at Wildflower 70.3.

In November 2009, she turned professional. Highlights include Ironman Canada 2010 champion, REV3 Portland 2011 1st place, Long Distance Triathlon World Championship 2011 3rd place, three 2nd place finishes, four 3rd place finishes, and three 4th place finishes.

2012 Schedule:
Ironman New Zealand (March)
Galveston 70.3 (or Oceanside) (April)
Ironman St. George (May)
EagleMan 70.3 (June)
Ironman Coeur d'Alene (June)
REV3 Portland (July)
Vineman 70.3 (July)
REV3 Dells (August)
Ironman Canada (August)
70.3 Worlds (September)
Kona, pending (October)
Ironman Arizona (November)

Professional Results:
2011

Ironman Arizona, 3rd Place Pro Female
Swim: 51:46 (2nd out of water) Bike: 4:53:36 (4th off the bike) Run: 3:10:18 (3rd runner)

Long Distance Triathlon WC, 3rd Place Pro Female
Swim: N/A Bike: 3:35:15 (TT start) Run: 2:03:54 (3rd runner)

REV3 Anderson, 3rd Place Pro Female
Swim: 25:24 (2) Bike: 2:33:39 (6) Run: 1:24:42 (3)

Ironman Wisconsin, 2nd Place Pro Female
Swim: 53:07 (1) Bike: 5:15:31 (1) Run: 3:34:51 (2)

Ironman Canada, 3rd Place Pro Female
Swim: 53:31 (1) Bike: 5:06:47 (2) Run: 3:33:40 (3)

Vineman 70.3, 4th Place Pro Female
Swim: 24:08 (2) Bike: 2:25:36 (3) Run: 1:25:33 (4)

REV3 Portland, 1st Place Pro Female
Swim: 26:60 (1) Bike: 2:20:47 (1) Run: 1:23:55 (1)

Texas 70.3, 8th Place Pro Female
Swim: 25:18 (3) Bike: 2:24:07 (10) Run: 1:25:05 (8)

2010
Ironman Arizona, 4th Place Pro Female
Swim: 51:21 (3rd out of water) Bike: 5:07:45 (3rd off the bike) Run: 3:11:32 (4th runner)

Ironman Canada, 1st Place Pro Female
Swim: 49:59 (2nd out of water) Bike: 5:09:33 (1st off the bike) Run: 3:10:14 (1st runner)

Ironman Coeur d'Alene, 2nd Place Pro Female
Swim: 54:07 (3rd out of water) Bike: 5:11:15 (2nd off the bike) Run: 3:14:23 (2nd runner)

Ironman St. George, 2nd Place Pro Female
Swim: 51:54 (3) Bike: 5:37:48 (2) Run: 3:12:40 (2)

New Orleans 70.3, 4th Place Pro Female
Swim: 29:00 (2) Bike: 2:22:35 (2) Run: 1:22: 24 (4)

2009
Ironman Arizona, 1st Pro Race, 7th Place Pro Female
Swim: 54:12 (3) Bike: 5:05:25 (3) Run: 3:32:50 (7)

Amateur/Age Group Results:
1st off the bike in all races, course records at Ironman Arizona and
Wildflower Long Course

Vineman 70.3, 1st Age Group
1st Overall Amateur
Swim: 25:18 Bike: 2:30:00 Run: 1:26:52

Ironman Coeur D'Alene, 1st Age Group
1st Overall Amateur, Hawaii Qualifier
Swim: 57:02 Bike: 5:21:57 Run: 3:36:19

Wildflower Long Course, 1st Age Group
1st Overall Amateur, Course Record
Swim: 25:56 Bike: 2:43:01 Run: 1:31:33

2008
Ironman Arizona, 1st Age Group
1st Overall Amateur, Hawaii Qualifier, Course Record
Swim: 52:35 Bike: 5:15:37 Run: 3:42:27

Ironman World Championship, Kona, 17th Age Group
Swim: 58:34 Bike: 5:52:33 Run: 3:53:16

Ironman Louisville, 1st Age Group
2nd Overall Amateur, Hawaii Qualifier
Swim: 55:37 Bike: 5:31:48 Run: 4:06:14

Vineman 70.3, 2nd Age Group
2nd Overall Amateur
Swim: 25:31 Bike: 2:41:27 Run: 1:29:25

Ironman Arizona, 2nd Age Group
Hawaii Qualifier
Swim: 55:03 Bike: 5:53:53 Run: 4:15:38

Coach:
Matt Dixon, purplepatch
Media:
Press Summary: www.meredithkessler.com/media.html
Twitter: twitter.com/mbkessler
Blog: www.meredithkessler.com/blog/

Sponsors:

<Include all of your current sponsor logos in this section>

I do not think you can ever be "too good" for a resume in the triathlon world, or in any athletic sport for that matter. Do not humbly hide your attributes; sponsors hear from everyone, and consequently, doors may be closed to you even with a very powerful resume. The majority of athletes in pro sports across the world (probably ninety-nine percent) have to compete to sell their brands. Only the elite athletes (Lebron James, David Beckham, Derek Jeter) who compete in a handful of sports (baseball, basketball, football, golf, soccer) truly have the autonomy to not have to sell themselves. They can go to any sponsors and work out very lucrative deals. The rest of us have to be very prepared when we approach sponsors. The resume is the first bit of information that identifies you to that sponsor, so make it count. It is tough to get a second chance to make a first impression.

Gear
I am not a gear head—never have been and never will be. This does not mean I am not excited to get a new bike or sleek Saucony running clothes. This means my attention isn't on what went into making what I use; I just want it to work, and I want to feel at ease with it. If what I

am using is reliable and I am on the path to attaining my goals, I am a happy athlete. I rarely read the new technology guides put out by *Triathlete Magazine* every year because I learn about what to use by watching others or by figuring out what feels comfortable to me. What I am trying to say is I may not be the authority on gear, but I have used a variety of equipment in my triathlon career spanning more than fifteen years, so I think I can provide a unique macro perspective on the situation.

Going into a season uncertain about your gear, especially about your bike or what you ingest during your training and races, is one of the worst things you can do. Of course I understand that complete certainty is not always possible. Sponsors may delay getting a number of products to you—including your bike—and there goes your off-season training! Practice with the products you can control, including gels, protein shakes, food, hydration, and whatever else you will be using on race day. You will never see a golfer play the Masters with a driver he has never used before, and the same should hold true for a triathlete. Consider the idea of trying out a new component system on your bike at Ironman St. George. Obviously it is not a very smart idea, yet it is a mistake I have done too many times in the past for the simple reason I *thought* I knew what I was doing—hubris took over.

The key is to practice as much as you can just like you would race on the day of your event. For some reason, triathletes are more prone than other athletes to try a new trick on race day that they overheard someone talking about at the athletes lounge the day before. Do your research before implementing a new product in your routine, and practice it multiple times to make sure it does not disrupt your foundation. If you have never eaten real potatoes on the bike leg of the triathlon, do not try it for the first time during your race. If you have never used gels during the run, do not experiment with it on mile eight of your big race. This may sound almost comical that I am mentioning this, but I am guilty of doing this far too often over my racing career, with very mixed results. I have also talked with both pros and amateurs who have had these same experiences. You do not want to play this game of Russian roulette.

The next worst thing you can do is sacrifice what works for sponsorship dollars. You graduate through the amateur ranks getting a basic understanding of what works for you and what does not, and you often end up with a lengthy array of different products you can use in every race. This comfort level is then tested when you become a pro through the contracts you negotiate and deals you develop with numerous sponsors. The company products you were comfortable with for your racing career may not be what you end up with as a pro, depending on what opportunities, if any, arrive at your doorstep.

There is a common misconception that pros have as much "stuff" as they want and have their choice of multiple products on the market. However, this is not the case, and pro athletes are wheeling and dealing to try to obtain the proper gear to help them succeed, just like the amateurs. What makes things more complicated is that pro athletes may have the opportunity to be with a triathlete team, who in turn has worked out exclusive sponsor deals for their athletes to use specific sponsor products. You may love the nutrition sponsor, but the bike sponsor's product just doesn't fit. I recently spoke to one of the best pro male bikers on the triathlon circuit who had joined a team whose bike sponsor did not have a frame that fit his body. He was riding in an extremely uncomfortable position, and it showed in his disappointing performance. He realized he had to request a break from the bike contract, which threatened his status with the team and sponsor money. The reality was, though, his current bike was costing him much more in confidence and future earnings.

I rode an Orbea bike when I was a successful amateur. It fit me perfectly, I knew how to handle it, and I liked the company. However, when I turned pro one of my sponsors had an exclusive deal with a different bike company, and consequently, I had to ride their model in my second pro race with minimal practice. Needless to say, the new bike and I were not compatible, and I had incorrectly let the money dictate my instinct. After a few costly lessons learned, I went back and renegotiated the contract to not include the bike. I then went to Orbea with a proposal. The results from my initial proposal weren't perfect. I first had to purchase a new Orbea and show them, through my racing, I was worth taking a chance on. It did have a happy ending, though.

They offered me a contract and reimbursed me for the Orbea I purchased (I will always be grateful to them for this). The moral of the story is although the money and contracts might be alluring, if they produce disappointing results, it may be more of a money drain on future race profits and podium incentives.

Another example is my running shoes. I ran in Nike shoes my entire life, but when I went pro, I knew I was not going to sign a multi-deal contract with the biggest shoe company in the world. I happened to forge a relationship with Saucony; they put their trust in me, and we worked out a partnership. I had limited time to try out their products. At this point, my decision was based on necessity. The first pair of shoes rubbed so badly that blisters developed after half a marathon; I was petrified. The next model, the Kinvara, worked perfectly, and the rest is history. They are now one of my favorite sponsors. I rate their product so high I recommend it to everyone. In both cases, I did not have the luxury of testing the product before races, which is a big red flag and should be avoided at all costs. In one case, it cost me a lot of money, and in another, I profited. The bottom line is to try your best to test everything you can in the off-season when the stakes are not as high.

My final thought on gear—and, to some extent, with triathlon in general—is to not over think things. Practice makes perfect—this is true in every sport. When the actual competition comes around, the motions will be second nature. There are so many aspects of the sport to think about in a race (which can be as long as sixteen hours), the brain would explode if you had to remember every little detail while racing. I have seen many triathletes fail because they were not prepared for the season and were nervous wrecks on race day. Inevitably something goes wrong, not because of a random occurrence, but because they did not prepare for their events. Pro golfer Phil Mickelson does not go out and miraculously play a seventy-two-course championship to perfection. He has practiced his sport so much that he is a few steps ahead of every shot he takes, his swing is effortless, and his body reacts to every situation placed in front of him. He has trained with these scenarios on the practice course a million times, and his body takes over. This is how the triathlete needs to approach his or her sport—so the pothole on mile seventy-eight of the bike is a small blip in the road, and the hot temperature is not even apparent.

Bike Fit

The bike fit is essential for any serious triathlete, amateur or pro. You are going to be spending a ridiculous amount of time on your bike seat, indoors and outdoors, and consequently, you have to make sure you are in an optimal position to increase performance and reduce injury. I usually get my bike properly fitted to me every off-season and, of course, whenever I receive a new bike from my sponsors. Not every type of bike fits the same, so you should get it professionally done for your triathlon, road, and mountain bike. Also, not every bike manufacturer fits the same, so if you switch brands, you need to get another bike fit.

As a triathlete, the most important aspects of the bike fit are to provide you with the ability to power through the longest of the three disciplines *and* to prepare you for the run. This second aspect is a key component because someone who is exclusively a cyclist does not need running legs after a bike ride, so the athlete's position on the bike is adjusted to maximize the power of the legs to propel the bike. However, if you are running any distance after your bike, you have to save some leg muscles for this activity or you risk premature fatigue or injury. A good bike fitter should know this and adjust your bike accordingly.

All too often I have seen triathletes, amateurs and pros, take an enormous amount of time, money, and travel to get a custom bike fit. The "show" is impressive. The bells and whistles of fancy equipment are in full effect. However, after months of riding, nagging injuries begin to develop in their legs, and their run performances are below their normal standards. Yes, their bike times may have dropped significantly, but the athletes are now in danger of serious injuries and have problems running. All of this strains their confidence. The theory is if you are now in a bike position that utilizes a lot of the same muscles you use on the run, the added strain can hurt your performance. Those leg muscles are precious. They need to be conditioned to run off the bike and still have enough reserves to propel you to the finish line. Therefore, it is crucial you get a proper bike fit and practice the bike to run in the off-season.

My bike measurements are included below from early in my professional career. I keep an electronic file with all of my past measurements for the bike fitter to analyze and to make sure it is on target with prior fittings. Too much of a dramatic change could lead to injury if not monitored properly.

Cyclist Name: Meredith Kessler
Make/Model: Orbea Ordu
Bike Fitting: April 22, 2011

Data Points:

A) Saddle height (cm) - 86
B) Saddle fore–aft (cm) - 3.8
C) Reach to rear of pads (cm)
From tip of saddle to rear of pads - 45.5
D) Bar drop to top of pads (cm)
From top of saddle to top of pads - 6
E) Saddle angle (degrees) - 2.7
F) Bar angle (degrees) - N/A

Crank length - 170
Pedal type - Shimano
Saddle type - ISM–Adamo
Shifter height - Shifter to floor - 91.6
Pad width - Center of each pad - 20
Pad reach - Rear of pad to shifter - 30.7
Virtual top tube length (c–c) (cm) - 52
Stem length (mm) - 70
Stem angle (degrees) - 0
Stem face up or down - N/A
Space between head tube and stem (cm) - 4.5
Handlebar width (c-c) (cm) - N/A
Ideal top tube length - 53

Appointment Notes:

Cleat placement: 44 laterally by 180

Shoes Size and Type: 39 Shimano

- Pad Reach: Current reach is 34.4. Shorten reach to shifters by 3.7cm for a 30.7 reach. This will eliminate the need to move your elbows from the rests to shift.
- Seat height: Raised seat by .6mm. Allows for greater leg extension. Currently I do not see your stability in the saddle being compromised. Let the height settle in and provide feedback.

Fits by Paul - Your Bike Fitter - www.fitsbypaul.com

These measurements may not mean much to the untrained eye, but to the bike technician, these millimeters and centimeters can determine if a rider is efficiently producing as much power as possible on the bike. In an Ironman distance, you can be on your bike between four and eight hours, so being uncomfortable during this immense amount of time can derail your chances of attaining your goals on race day. You should not gloss over the bike fit; it would be like buying an uncomfortable bed, which leads to nights of tossing and turning. You awake unrefreshed and ill prepared for your day. The bike fit is the same way. If it is done properly, it will allow for maximum output in all facets of the triathlon; if it is done poorly, good luck trying to push through the race at your peak and improving your finishing times.

Paul Kundrat has performed my bike fit in San Francisco, and I have used him, at times, since I was competing as an amateur. He is one of the top technicians in the industry, and he is local, so this is the perfect situation for me. Additionally, his prices are reasonable, and he comes to my home for the fitting. I have recently used Paul Buick from New Zealand. There is no one out there who is as knowledgeable and caring about his craft and I owe a lot to him in improving my overall bike times.

A professional fitting is well worth the cost because your livelihood and performance depends on it. There are many pros that travel all over the world to work with some of the leaders in this industry. It has become such an exact science that precision equipment, wind tunnels, and computers are now all tools used by the top-notch facilities. When you are looking to cut minutes off of your bike time, every millimeter counts, so the bike fitter's skill is a commodity.

A great bike fitter does not have to use the latest and greatest in scientific technology. However, I cannot stress enough, if you are a triathlete, find a fitter who understands the concept of running off of the bike and can implement this idea in your personal fit. If you are going to a new bike fitter and there is an enormous change in your overall positioning, this should be an immediate red flag. You might be way out of whack with your existing fit, but you should ease into your optimal fit over time, not in one day. The risk of injury is too great. You will inevitably work muscles you were not working before, which can result in multiple problems, such as overcompensation and fatigue, especially if you ride as hard after the fit as you did before it. The goal of a professional bike fit is to dramatically reduce your times by putting your body in the best position to bike and run off the bike. Be aware of the danger of trying to reach those levels haphazardly.

Training

If you are reading this book, I assume you either have an idea of what your training program should be, or you are researching to discover one that works with your schedule. This manual would be hundreds of pages longer if I tried to tackle all of the workouts I have used in my triathlon-racing career. Instead of providing general workouts, this is an overview of how to train. By envisioning yourself at the end of next season, you can start to figure out what you need to do during the off-season to get there.

The first step is to look yourself in the mirror and give an honest review of your year. Did you accomplish what you set out to achieve? Did you have an effective balance of training, family, and friends in your life? Did you earn the income you expected from racing or other sources? Write out your achievements and failings, and determine what you can improve on in your life, triathlon, and training. This may sound like something you have heard throughout your life, but how many people actually do it? This list will pinpoint your strengths and weaknesses. It will give you an idea of what you need to work through in the off-season and provide a path for the upcoming season.

The next step is to evaluate your coach. In her book, *A Life Without Limits: A World Champion's Journey*, Chrissie Wellington relates that she had a stretch of three coaches and experimented with self-coaching. She makes it easy to understand how a person can develop a relationship with a coach, and then move on as new circumstances arise; it was all part of her journey to grow and maintain her elite racing. Your first coach might not be your last one, and, just like a lot of relationships, you might grow apart or need to separate to mature in other facets of your racing. Evaluating your coach may seem like a dramatic step in your racing career, but if you treat your athletic career like a business, your coach is simply an employee overseeing one of your most important divisions. Employees get evaluations every year, and your coach should be no different. Employees also get replaced for a multitude of reasons, good or bad, so this is a distinct possibility with every evaluation.

You should have an end of the year talk with your coach to discuss your performance last season and the goals you already outlined for next year. Determine if you actually had the season you expected and, if not, who was at fault. If you look in the mirror, you should be objective about determining if you failed yourself or if your coach did not live up to your expectations. Remember, it is easy to pass the blame onto someone else, but only you can figure out if your coach has the right philosophy and personality to get the most out of you. Did you follow his or her program, or did you deviate with your own philosophy? Were you constantly tinkering with other methods and not following the coach's advice completely?

If you followed your coach's program and still underachieved, it might make sense to explore other options. If you realize you had your hands in your own training without giving your coach a chance, then you probably meddled in your own development. Triathletes have Type A personalities and find it tough to give complete control over their training to their coaches. Objectively look to see if you, as owner of your business, let your employee, the coach, do his or her job, or if you thought you knew what was best and altered the plan. I have coached many athletes who say they are following my plan to appease me, and then I discover they are tacking on additional bike rides, swims, or running sessions, which puts my overall plan in jeopardy.

If the relationship was a productive one and you met your goals for the season, it is logical to continue on the journey with your present coach. Do not mess with success. Finding a coach you believe in is a large part of the equation, because it instills a confidence that is otherwise hard to attain. Why do you think coaches such as Pat Riley, Nick Saban, or Pat Summitt are so revered in their profession? The attitude and confidence they project on their teams is unparalleled and not easily duplicated. This holds true with a strong triathlon coach because you rely on him or her to prepare you for race day. Discuss with your coach what worked and where you need improvement, and be comfortable with the plan that he or she has in place for the off-season. At this point, you should have some semblance of what your race schedule looks like, so your coach can plan the training and consequent evolution accordingly.

My last piece of advice for off-season training is to take the time to improve your weaknesses. This is the point in your journey when you can work on new things and get better. I receive requests from amateurs during the course of the year asking for a few tips on what to do in the off-season, and I tell them to model their regimen on high-profile athletes' off-seasons: they look to improve the weakest parts of their discipline so they come back a more well-rounded competitor. Do you think Shaun White practices his same tricks in the half-pipe in the off-season? No, he learns new tricks and irons out the wrinkles in his overall presentation. Do you think Lebron James works on his dunking, a skill he mastered in high school? This would not make him a better player. Instead, he works on his post game with his back to the basket so he can add another skill to his repertoire.

As a triathlete, you have to master three distinct disciplines with their own idiosyncrasies, so the work is never complete. If your bike to run is where you lose a lot of time, practice intervals of long bike rides and speed runs to strengthen these muscles. If you never swam growing up and your swimming is not on par with your competitors, join a swim group and push yourself. Get creative and swim with the local high school team to get some structured repetition. If your nutrition is a mystery and you are continually throwing up during races, experiment with different fuel during your training sessions to determine what works best for you. Target certain areas of your race skill set so you can look back the next year and determine if you actually improved on those aspects you planned to conquer.

At the beginning of 2011, I set out to get faster on the marathon portion of the Ironman. I was competitive, but the overall pro women times were dropping dramatically. Mirinda Carfrae set the bar high with consistent sub-three-hour performances in high-profile Ironman races, and she was only going to get better in her other disciplines. I worked with my former coach to create an off-season training program to produce better speed on the run. I also entered quite a few sprint races to train my muscles to go faster. The results were my run time did improve, but the biggest gain was in my 70.3 racing where the speed came in handy. The point is I did not set out to get better at every part of my racing. I concentrated on a few flaws that I worked on correcting through a targeted training program developed between my coach and me.

EQUIPMENT AND GEAR

I will not approach this chapter like a typical gear guide you would find in a triathlon publication. *Triathlete Magazine* and *Lava Magazine* do a tremendous job diagramming the latest and greatest equipment in cycling, running, and swimming, so there is no added value for me to drone on about a subject the experts have already tackled. Triathletes love gear, and they will research the heck out of it in order to get what they want. I admit, I am always partial to my sponsors because I know their products the best, but technology seems to keep pace between companies, similar to the ski industry. A top-of-the-line ski might have a few modifications that make it conducive to one body type over another, but personal preference truly separates it from another ski. The performance will be very similar (I am sure some product manufacturers will disagree with me on this point), and it is up to the athlete to make it work correctly.

Equipment is all mental. What I mean by this is if you have a positive experience with a bike, you will be sold on that product, but if you have a bad experience, your confidence in the bike will diminish. If I have a fly rod and lose a fish, my subconscious might blame the rod even though I am just a subpar fisherman. If I wipe out on the ski slope and have a horrible crash, mentally I will not push as hard on those skis the next few runs, or maybe I will not push as hard ever again. My confidence has been shot. If you are comfortable with a bike when you start your triathlon experience, you will probably stick with this brand. This is why sponsors work hard to get in front of new triathletes through promotions with their pro athletes. These customers are the most valuable ones because they are with them for life.

Fellow pro Melanie McQuaid wrote one of the best blog posts I have read about the psychological effects of equipment on the racer. It was a cold, blustery day for Ironman Oceanside 2012, and Melanie passed me effortlessly in a technical bike section on her way to an impressive victory. I was in awe as she navigated the route as if the bike were an extension of her brain, fluidly biking by me as if I were encrusted in cement. After the race she described her performance in her blog, and her words portray someone who is so in tune with her equipment that the confidence oozes from the text. This is someone who was at the top of her game, and all it took was faith in a new bike to push her to a new level. Please note this is NOT a promotion of Trek or any of her other sponsors as many professionals will have the same positive experience with the gear they use; it is an example of how equipment can affect the athlete in a positive way.

Excerpt from Melanie McQuaid's blog (www.racergirl.com):
I couldn't be more thrilled to start off the 2012 season with my partners with the biggest 70.3 win of my career. How great is that to give your supporters a boost in confidence right off the bat, huh? I have had some confidence that I have been keeping somewhat quiet as I slowly built my form toward this season. To be honest, I wasn't thinking that I could win given how strong the field was in Oceanside and I was just starting my season. To nab the top spot on the podium was the most killer feeling that came entirely unexpectedly. But I think you need some background to understand why this win is so special to me.

First, I would like to thank the incredible female professionals who pushed me so hard on Saturday that I managed to crush my own time from last year's race by twelve minutes. Heather Jackson created a great battle before taking second—thank you and wow you are so talented and undoubtedly have many successful years ahead of you. To Meredith Kessler in third, you are a class act—it was so inspiring to even catch you out there after such a fast swim! Rachel McBride from Canada, who also rode a Trek Speed Concept to the second fastest bike time in Oceanside, had a breakthrough race to eventually hold fourth place overall. Congratulations to my teammates Linsey Corbin and XTERRA World Champion Lesley Paterson who rode their Trek Speed Concept to fifth and sixth place on the day…

I have struggled a bit since I came into my first Half Ironman distance race a few years ago, as I felt my race results didn't reflect my fitness, particularly on the bike. This disconnect with my cycling ability, to a certain extent, would carry over into the run. But really, I am not a runner anyways, I need to ride fast to win. I like to take personal responsibility for that and tried a number of different bike fits, setups, and training strategies on my time trial bike to try to address the weakness, but it wasn't really coming together. It was kind of frustrating, and I struggled with whether I just wasn't good on the road. Not much was really working out until I had a chat with Trek.

When Trek sent me a Speed Concept my reality changed. Not only did I instantly and naturally find the position that was right for me, the metrics in that new position were a revelation. I didn't radically change my training over the winter and my numbers, although good right now, are not the best in my career in absolute terms. They are incredible when compared to what I used to do on a time trial bike the past few years and just shows how fast that bike is especially when I feel comfortable on it. Improving on last year's split at Oceanside 70.3 by eight minutes, in what I thought were tougher conditions, is one hundred percent clarification that Trek is where it is at. This decision and opportunity is absolutely a game changer and I couldn't be more stoked about it. That was my fifth ride outdoors on the bike and three of them were on the bike path riding easy in a straight line. There is a lot of room for improvement, especially technically, and that has me pretty fired up.

…There were some other decisions to make over the winter. I went through my program to decide what would TRULY make me faster and made decisions accordingly. Any new partners were brought in to improve the program and the things that were working really well were preserved…

Let's do our best to kick it up a notch this season, why don't we. There is much unfinished business that must be addressed.
End

*

A pro athlete's process for choosing a particular sponsor is never black and white. A lot goes into negotiating sponsorships, figuring out which companies can coexist, and factoring money in the equation. Sponsor A could be your best bet for performance on the bike, but their money might already be invested in other athletes. You then have to weigh the value of going with Sponsor B, which pays more money, yet could ultimately lose you podium dollars.

How Melanie and other triathletes come to their decisions to go with a sponsor depends on many circumstances. Money plus forged relationships plus performance plus time does not always equal or create the optimal setup for you to succeed. Each component factors into the gear you have on race day and hopefully your training and confidence in the products will allow you to achieve your goals. Nothing is worse than *not* trusting your equipment.

I created a list below of all of the products I use in the sport of triathlon, how I arrived at the decision to use these products, and why I am confident in them. These products will probably have changed by the time this book is published because the sponsorship world is in constant motion to try to find that magical formula. However, I use these products as examples because, at the time, many different factors came together to form the right combination of performance, confidence, and money.

Gear used as of December, 2012

Bike—Orbea

A pro tennis player can try out every racquet on the market before deciding which to use in competition. An amateur or pro triathlete usually does not have the luxury of trying out several different bikes because of the amount of time it takes to get dialed in on one, let alone the twenty or more brands on the market. I rode an Orbea as an amateur because it was the first high-end bike I tried, it did not break down, and I was successful on it. Another high-end bike I used was constantly in the shop, which reduced my overall confidence with the discipline. I hounded Orbea with phone calls and emails to try work out a partnership because I did not want to go through the time-consuming process of finding another bike that I had confidence in. The persistence paid off and Orbea and I developed a partnership.

Bike Transport—TriBike Transport (TBT)

In reality, there are not too many options to transport your bike. You can pack it yourself and send it on the plane, but when it arrives, you have to rebuild it, and I do not have those skills. This all costs time and money. TBT was one of my first sponsors, and I will always be thankful to them for taking a chance on a rookie. They are a local San Francisco company, which is how I heard about them and met the owner. I have never had a problem with their service, and they now work with all the Ironman pro triathletes.

Clothing, Shoes, Kit—Saucony
Linsey Corbin introduced me to the Saucony athlete representative at Ironman Arizona, my first race as a pro. We hit it off, and I made the switch from wearing my Nike clothes to Saucony. I have not looked back. This is the rare combination where the product was impeccable, the stipend was right, and the timing was perfect!

Coaching—purplepatch
This is not physical equipment, but it is definitely a component of triathlon. Some pro triathletes take years to find a coach that will help them reach their goals, and others change quite often. They take what was helpful to them from their previous coach and apply it to their next endeavor. It was the right place and time for purplepatch owner Matt Dixon and me to begin our journey together. His coaching style is all I have ever known, and it works for both of us. We are not only a coach-athlete team, but we have become good friends through this relationship.

Components, Bike Shoes—Shimano
This is a company I actually did my research on and realized that their components were extremely well liked in the industry, especially the Di2 system. I met the Shimano contact at Interbike in Las Vegas in 2009 and kept in contact over the years. They run a team, which I could not be a part of because my existing partnerships clashed with theirs. The result was we struck an informal agreement where I advertise on their behalf, and they try to provide me with product.

Cycling—ShiftSF
Once again, this is not equipment, but it is such a big component of my training, it has to be included. I live in a city with a fitness-centric

attitude, so there is no shortage of cycling studios. I was referred to ShiftSF by a friend, and there I developed close relationships, met my coach, and now teach cycling classes.

Fuel, Racing Belt—T1

The owner emailed me persistently for several months before I decided to try his belt, which I use when I run. He did a special monogram for me and even adjusted it to my specifications. He received what he wanted, which was someone to not only try but also advertise his product during races. I teamed with a partner and product that benefitted me, plus I could give feedback to a receptive manufacturer.

Glasses, Helmets—Rudy Project

A friend on the Everyman Jack triathlon team provided me with the sponsor contact, and I sent him a cover email and resume. We have since signed a contract, and I could not be more pleased with the quality of the glasses and helmet.

Power, Trainers—CycleOps/PowerTap

Matt Dixon at purplepatch negotiated a deal with CycleOps to promote their product, and then he got me in touch with the representative. Using Power changed my whole attitude on the bike. I had a tendency to drift in my focus, and riders would sneak up on me as my watts reduced. Power enabled me to stay on top of my game throughout the bike portion; it kept me at a consistent pace and helped me not get overtaken because I was not paying attention. The problem you will run into with bike frames and tools associated with the bike is sometimes they do not sync well. For instance, the Power does not work with the top-of-the-line Reynolds wheels, the RZRs, consequently, I have not been able to ride with them. I have to sacrifice aerodynamics for the ability to monitor my watts.

Seat—ISM

Everyone seems to ride on ISM seats. This was my initial thought as an amateur looking for sponsors. I became fast friends with the owner after meeting him at events and was eager to strike up a partnership. They do a tremendous job of marketing their product and the pro athletes that use their product.

Tires—Challenge

I did not have a tire sponsor my first two years as a pro. I did not know how much pressure to use, what tires were best, what size tread I should use, and when to change out. The money I spent on tires and the mishmash of brands I used was way out of line. Janelle Kellman, owner of Kit Order, overheard my dilemma and introduced me to the Challenge representative. The knowledge I have gained in dealing with an expert on tires is more than worth the partnership. The amazing product is a bonus.

Recovery—Recovery Pump

I met the contact at a product forum at an Ironman race. They convinced me of the value of their system—how it could help my legs recover and prepare me for races. They sold me the unit at cost. Once I had experimented with the boots and was happy with the results, I immediately reached out to discuss a partnership. Eventually, they came out for a photo shoot to use in their marketing and reimbursed me the cost I initially paid. I am now a happy affiliate sponsor: I get paid for any unit sold through the link on my website. By the way, I use the boots all the time. They are terrific, as I explain in later chapters!

Watch—Timex

I met the Timex representative at Interbike as a wide-eyed amateur trying to get into the pro ranks. Once again, they already had a team in place, so I did not look to them for sponsorship. However, we kept in contact and eventually laid out an informal agreement to wear their product, which is free advertising for them.

Web Design—Eminess Design

This is not equipment, but it is imperative you enter into a trusted relationship with your web designer. Your website is your primary marketing tool for you and your sponsors. Matt Sterling is a friend who also happens to be a talented designer and the owner of Eminess Design, so it was a right place, right time situation when he agreed to work with me on my web designs.

Weight Training—TRX

They are another Bay Area-based company, and I started using the device at ShiftSF. They went on a huge marketing push before Kona a few years ago and partnered with multiple triathletes to discuss their product on social media. I was lucky enough to have met the athlete representative at TRX and got wind from other athletes they were offering contracts. I immediately reached out to them, since it is one of my favorite exercise tools, and signed an agreement. Their marketing blitz clearly paid off. They were a little-known company trying to make headway in the triathlon community, so they threw marketing dollars at the challenge and were catapulted into the limelight. If you ever have a chance to ride a train like this, leap at the opportunity.

Wetsuit—Orca

I had used XTERRA wetsuits as an amateur and my first few races as a pro. However, Orbea was in an agreement with Orca which stated any pro athlete under contract on an Orbea bike had to wear an Orca wetsuit. These partnerships were once quite common in the industry, but they have decreased because of the inflexibility it places on the athlete. Biking is the longest part of the race, so it was an easy decision to go with Orbea and Orca rather than stay with XTERRA and look for another bike sponsor. Orca and XTERRA both served me well.

Wheels—Reynolds Cycling

When I worked at RBC Capital Markets, a partner who knew I did triathlons approached me and gave me the contact information for the owner of Reynolds Wheels. He was a childhood friend of the partner, who was kind enough to offer the information to a new pro. This was the lead I needed to get my foot in the door and eventually meet the whole crew while at Interbike. They were looking to tap the triathlon market, and I made the pitch that I was the one to do it. The lesson is that you never know where a good lead will come from, so network, network, network.

Equipment and Gear Addendum—February, 2013

What a difference a few months makes during sponsorship negotiation season. We made it a point to find different partners this offseason in the pursuit of faster gear, solid contracts that coincide with a successful 2012 season, and long-term partners so that we wouldn't have to negotiate as many contracts in 2014. As with any offseason, the goal is to improve, and this includes the equipment used for training and racing. It was with much regret I parted ways with some longtime partners but "I" am a business, and I am always looking to optimize my ability to race well, which includes gear and improving the bottom line: income.

The purpose of adding an addendum to the end of this chapter is to show how quickly what you are using as a pro triathlete can change, as well as why the decision was made. The negotiations were intense during a brief three-week period when we learned a main sponsor, unbeknownst to us, was going in a different direction. There is also the fact that contracts expire on December 31, and athletes can then announce they are changing companies, freeing up money for others.

Triathlon sponsorship is an unusual process because most sponsors do not pursue the athletes. If you are John Daly and hit the ball a long ways, golf club makers will be lining up to work with you. If you can swim really fast, it doesn't mean you will get a call from a wetsuit company; you have to market yourself and be persistent. A contract is rarely a reflection of past results and a raise based on performance is tough to come by. The majority of the feedback we received is the money is tied up with other individuals or the company had no budget.

Aerodynamic Hydration and Storage—Xlab USA
The bike has always been a pain point with me through my age group and pro careers. This offseason, I sought out partners to improve aerodynamics. It was with great surprise that Xlab reached out to me to inquire about a partnership; they were one of the only companies to do this. I already used their products, and now I have them as a partner to bounce ideas off of to figure out the best way to store my hydration and nutrition on the bike.

Bike—Cannondale
The saga of finding a bike partner was daunting. Our previous sponsor made some last minute changes that required all of their athletes to be in their kit. We were told this at an unfortunate time late in the season. Luckily, we knew there were going to be companies that would do this

because it has happened for the past three years, so we have kept an open dialogue with a lot of prospective bike companies. We targeted what we considered the fastest bikes on the market with the goal being able to partner with a tremendous company and quality bike. After negotiating with a handful of companies, we decided Cannondale was the place to be, and we are eager to begin our partnership with them.

Component Lubrication—Atomic High Performance
We were fortunate to have a friend in the industry pass along the contact information for Atomic. Their revolutionary lubricant and sealing systems reduce drag in components making your bike faster. We met the owner, Andy Weathers, and he is a cyclist and triathlete. We discovered we were on the same wavelength and look forward to working with him. It is a fact: you will be hearing more about the rise of Atomic in the near future.

Earbuds—Yurbuds
In Kona, in addition to racing, Aaron and I used the opportunity to pass out business cards at the booths of companies where there was a potential to partner in 2013. Yurbuds was high on my list because I use their buds during training and before races. We met with them and are now happy to be part of their team.

Wetsuit—ROKA Sports
It was a stroke of luck and fate that we were able to partner with ROKA after our wetsuit/bike sponsor sprung unfortunate news on us in late November. They sold us on their swimming and business backgrounds, their vision for the company, and the revolutionary design of their wetsuit. We love partnering with up and coming, innovative companies, and ROKA fits this mold.

Wheels—Enve Components
We reached out to multiple wheel companies to keep our options open since our current contract was up at the end of 2012. We have learned, no matter how good a relationship you have with a company, it is a business and anything can happen during contract negotiation time. Enve was a company we have always heard great things about from trusted sources within the bike industry, so we were ecstatic when they

came back to us with an unbelievable offer we could not pass up. The wheels are fast and built to last.

Equipment and Gear Addendum—February, 2016

Your gear and equipment is an evolution. This is the best word to describe how a professional and age group triathlete should navigate the immense field of products. As you can see from my experience, you start off naïve, gain some knowledge and make smarter decisions, and then come to a place where you can target, more effectively and efficiently, what you need to help perform at your best. The bottom line, you want to get faster and if equipment helps you do this, make the change!

As I had success in triathlon and was able to grow my brand, we were able to partner with companies that benefitted us both. After many races, I know what works for me and what does not and this knowledge allowed me to target certain businesses. We also started focusing on companies that were out of the triathlon community niche to further expand into different facets of society; the goal was to find partners outside of the extremely competitive arena of triathlon. We wanted to introduce outside companies to triathlon, and in turn, have them introduce our brand to their arena. As I stated before, you need to evolve or you will plateau.

Bike—Ventum

Good things come to those who wait. This is a phrase you do not hear too often in the world of professional triathlete sponsorship negotiations; usually it is the early bird gets the worm! After multiple years of working with multiple bike companies, I was finally in a position where I had a few offers on the table. The most intriguing one was Ventum, the Ferrari of bike industry and new kid on the block. In reality, we had known about Ventum for awhile since we were friends with the owner for many years. The stars now aligned where we were free agents and they were looking for athletes to ride their machine. I signed with Ventum knowing that I was now on an extremely fast bike (my wind tunnel tests were all the proof I needed), and an amazing support crew who would work tirelessly to make sure I was ready to go for each race.

Component and Bearings—Ceramic Speed
In the endless pursuit to find speed, Ceramic Speed is on the top of the list of adjustments an athlete can make to improve performance. It is what we call 'free speed'! I started working with them in 2014 when I built up my Enve wheels with Ceramic Speed wheel bearings. We then worked in the bottom bracket and pulley wheels. You can really see the difference with each added piece of gear as to why they are so sought after by professional and age group athletes.

Education—Play2Health
As professional triathletes get older, they realize that you cannot race forever. This leads some to seek out different avenues such as coaching, speaking, training, etc…They also seek ways to give back whether it be through charity or education. Play2Health is designed to promote good exercise habits and fitness education; we want to get children off the couch and their computer devices and outside playing. We want to stop the epidemic of obesity in the world by stressing the importance of play and how this has become a lost art.

Energy—Red Bull
There are certain times where working with a company becomes an absolute pleasure for the athlete. Red Bull has created a powerful company, strategic marketing machine, athletic empire, and valuable, entertaining, and informative content. I had been speaking with them for two years before entering into a formal agreement in 2014. They do their best to help make sure their athletes succeed which is why it is such a joy to work with their team. They wanted to get into triathlon and promote the benefits of the Red Bull product in training and racing. As I always say, Red Bull helps propel you to the finish line and it is better than the sugar water served at some races. They support us with training camps, speaking engagements, contests, and educational exercises.

Granola—Bungalow Munch
Eating Bungalow Munch is as regular in my daily routine as brushing my teeth. My day begins with a banana, yogurt, and Bungalow Munch on top of the yogurt. Throughout the day, I nibble on it to keep my

energy up, metabolism moving, and to provide me with quality nutrition and fuel. Bungalow Munch granola was created and is made by my good friend Jeri Howland. She is a mother, wife, professional, and multiple Ironman champion so she knows what it takes to keep an active individual going throughout the day. My daily routine changed for the better a few years ago when I was introduced to this wonderful food and I want to thank Jeri for creating it.

Health Food— ZÜPA Noma

As I mentioned before, the advantage of growing your brand in the sport of triathlon is that you might get the opportunity to work with new and upcoming companies. I was fortunate to know the founder of ZÜPA through my Bay Area triathlon friends. There is a growing movement towards natural, healthy, and fresh meals and ZÜPA will be at the forefront of this movement. In a nutshell, it is healthy, cold soup you find in the refrigerated section. As endurance athletes, we consistently run hungry around the clock. We are constantly searching for the secret sauce and that perfect, healthy, tasty, and nutritious food item that we can incorporate into our daily regimen. ZÜPA is one of those marquee items that can be consumed multiple times a day for your overall healthy benefit. It is also a simple and enjoyable way to get your vegetables!

Recovery and Immune Health—Vector450

As you grow older, recovery and good health becomes tough to practice and maintain. For this reason, I was sold on the beneficial qualities of Vector450 after Ironman Arizona 2014. I immediately used it after the race, through Challenge Bahrain, and Ironman Auckland 70.3. What I noticed right away is it helped my 'swollenness' after a race, assisted in my recovery, and was instrumental in helping shelter me from the loads of germs around in the US winters and while traveling from event to event.

Software—Kit Order

I have known owners Janelle Kellman and Kate Ligler (also my personal trainer) for years and they have always been innovative business women. They are one of the leaders in the industry to create white labeled platforms tailored to meet a clients branding and business needs for direct to consumer sales. It's tremendous to partner with innovative software companies headed by female leaders in the San Francisco Bay Area.

Wearable Technology—Lumo Run

I began talking to Lumo in 2013 about their plans for a running application, to not only keep statistics, but actually improve your running form. We stayed in touch and I was hired to consult during the beginning stages of the product and information gathering. As the device was formulated through countless hours of testing, gaining knowledge, and trial and error, it became evident that a very helpful product was developing. I continue to work with Lumo Run with the official launch coming in the 2nd half of 2016. There are a lot of devices that monitor information but nothing on the market that coaches and corrects inadequacies in your running form. The sky is the limit with how Lumo Run can help runners reduce injury and improve times.

NUTRITION, HYDRATION, FUELING, AND RECOVERY

Even though my major in college was nutrition, no other aspect of the sport has given me more problems than figuring out my nutrition, hydration, and fueling. When you are competing at the highest level in this sport, any miscalculation can have dire consequences. Finishing and making it to the podium or passing out at mile twenty of the run can be the difference between eating that last gel off of the bike or taking the extra time to stop and drink some Red Bull when your competitor is within sight. Unfortunately, trial and error has cost me a few high-profile podium finishes and lots of dollars. As I stated in the opening prologue, there is no substitution for race day experience, but you can race smarter to try to avoid some of the inevitable pitfalls that afflict all triathletes through their racing careers. I hope you can take tidbits from my experiences and setbacks to help you safely finish your next race.

Hydration

The best way to discuss these subjects is by first defining them, starting with hydration. Everyone knows you should hydrate steadily over the course of a day, and you need to increase this before, during, and after workouts. The problem is there is no one-size-fits-all manual for hydration; everyone is different. Pro triathlete Maik Twelsiek steps outside on a hot day and immediately is drenched in sweat. He has trouble taking in all of the liquids he needs on a hot race day because of how his body excretes fluids. I have had problems with my kidneys because of my high sweat rate and my difficulty in properly hydrating for extended periods of time. When I worked behind a desk for fifty to sixty hours a week, my focus was on my job, and I was lax about hydrating. Subconsciously, I think I also was annoyed with getting up and peeing every fifteen minutes in the office setting. I can only call it "binge water drinking," which any nutritionist will tell you, is not an effective way to hydrate. I would remember to hydrate at odd times during the course of the day and gulp down twenty ounces of water, which ultimately flows right through your body.

There are many factors to consider when deciding how much fluid to have during a race. These include the temperature, humidity, altitude, and energy output. These, along with your body weight and sweat rate, compose the complicated equation of hydration while racing. You can find out the majority of this information before exerting yourself, except for sweat rate, which I do recommend ascertaining for any serious athlete. I took a sweat test because of my hydration troubles and discovered that my hydration level was low. I should have been taking in seventeen milliliters of fluid per minute, which equates to roughly a mouthful of liquid, when I was only taking in eight milliliters per minute. This was an almost two to one loss ratio. From this I learned my fluid loss rate is higher than the average female, and I was not absorbing enough fluid to properly counterbalance this loss.

Another readily used equation is to drink at least one ounce of water for every pound of your body weight. This establishes your baseline for hydration *before* you calculate the liquid you need while training. If you research and prepare your hydration by systematically combining all of these factors, you will save years of trial and error in the hydration battle fought by every endurance athlete.

I am still working on deciphering all of these different aspects of hydration, as evidenced by my race in 2012 at the Ironman World Championship 70.3 in Las Vegas. I was overcoming a back injury at the time and was concentrating on that. Consequently, I forgot to follow the proper steps for hydration before the race. I went from training in seventy degree San Francisco weather to working out in ninety-five degree temperatures in Las Vegas and did not adjust my hydration. I also was traveling to and from professional triathlete responsibilities, and I neglected drinking the proper fluids en route and during these events. This, combined with my increased intake of ibuprofen to four to six pills per day for a month to handle my back pain, left me in a very dehydrated state. It reared its ugly head halfway through the bike as my power significantly dropped, and then the run became a death march. My lapse in handling my hydration responsibility is even more irritating to me because I am very aware of my kidney issues and know

I have to stay on top of this aspect of my training. At this time, I was almost a four-year pro with over ten years of experience, and I still made elementary mistakes that impeded my racing. Hopefully you can learn from my errors.

Knowing that the body is a complex instrument and each of us will follow different paths to perform at our best, I offer the following suggestions on hydration.

- Hydration should become part of your daily routine, like brushing your teeth or eating. You should get to the point where you don't think about it, you just do it—it is that important.
- Keep a bottle of water at your desk while you are working.
- Sip liquids throughout the day; try to avoid binge drinking.
- Do not fear the many trips to the bathroom. It is an inevitable consequence of proper hydration.
- You should try to make the drinking experience pleasant so it will not be a chore to consume. I have a SodaStream machine that injects carbonation into water, which I, find easier to drink. I also like to use a straw when drinking my liquids because, for some reason, it helps me to drink more over the course of a day.
- Keep liquid by your bed during the night. If you feel the least bit parched, you have readily available liquid to consume. This is especially important the night before a race.
- You should consume one ounce of water per pound of body weight, so a 130-pound person should drink 130 ounces of liquid. This does not include exercise. Your total intake when training should be much higher.
- Keep hydrating drinks in your car. Availability is the key here. Be ready with liquids when you are stuck in traffic or go on that long drive across town.
- You need to drink before, during, and after workouts. I know this is obvious, but I hear a lot of excuses triathletes give for not having proper hydration during workouts.
- Do not forget to hydrate race week; it can slip your mind if you get consumed by the hoopla surrounding the event. This includes drinking sixteen ounces every hour on the airplane

flight, sipping steadily throughout the days leading up to the race, and properly replenishing after pre-race workouts.

- There is no substitute for water. You can consume a lot of electrolyte and sports drinks, but doctors will tell you there is no replacing drinking a steady stream of water throughout the day.
- Research the conditions surrounding your training regimen or race. This includes taking note of the weather (humid, hot, cold, etc.), altitude, and how much energy you will spend. This will be an indicator of the amount of liquid you should bring and consume over the course of the event.
- Keep an eye on your pee. If it is a darker color, you are dehydrated. If it is clear, you have liquids coming through your body at a fast rate. If it is lightly colored, you are probably hydrated.
- If you have a workout that is less than an hour, drink when you are thirsty.

I preach hydrating as much as possible because I have a tough time getting the adequate fluids in my body for it to perform properly. I am constantly searching for ways to increase and maintain my liquid intake, and I do think a high percentage of athletes are in this same category. Life gets in the way of proper hydration. However, you should also be aware there is a condition called overhydration, or water intoxication, where the body contains too much water. This can occur during intense workouts or on race day when you take in more water than you are excreting. The other factor that can occur is your electrolytes and sodium become too diluted, which can result in a number of debilitating side effects. I learned about overhydration through my years of improperly hydrating myself, which ended up affecting my kidneys. I have to really concentrate on my hydration, along with monitoring my sodium and electrolyte intake, especially on race day. The moral is you need to find the proper balance for your body to achieve peak performance.

Nutrition

Nutrition is a topic that is so broad and time consuming it would take a separate manual to even scratch the surface. There are so many opinions, articles, and studies on the subject that you can become lost in an endless sea of information. I view nutrition as what I consume, throughout the course of the day, to keep my body functioning properly. Nutrition, combined with vitamins and supplements, if done correctly, allows me to compete at my peak level more often than not. I enjoy discovering and creating healthy meals that provide me with the pleasure of eating what I like, while achieving the best nutritional benefits. The repertoire of quality meals I enjoy has steadily increased enough over the years to provide me with a rotation of food that brings me satisfaction and proper health benefits.

I love food and wine. There is nothing that gives me greater pleasure than going to our favorite restaurant, Hillstone (I know it is a chain, but it is quality food every time), bringing a bottle of wine (there is no corkage fee), and enjoying the smoked salmon and seared tuna salad. Occasionally, we order the sundae as a decadent treat. These experiences are what life is about—combining good company with a tasty wine that pairs with my favorite foods perfectly. I am not one to completely restrict what I eat because I enjoy the taste and experience way too much; it is a way of life. My life would be much less enjoyable if I followed the philosophy that food is just to fuel the body and is an emotionless activity used only to get me through the day.

With that said, you need to be smart about what you eat, or other areas of your life will suffer. I equate nutrition to preventative medicine. An individual may take pills to prevent clogged arteries but not see the results right away. However, the medication can prolong this person's life. Nutrition is the same way. You do not see the immediate damage a bad diet will do to your body, but eventually, it will come back to haunt you. The same is true for a smart diet. Your immediate training might not be affected, but you will be thankful for your intelligent nutritional diet on the run leg of the triathlon.

It is a cliché, however, moderation directly correlates to a positive nutritional experience. You can be a triathlete and not meticulously monitor everything you put into your body. You can have that glass of wine, dessert, potato chip, or pizza, but do not go overboard and let these types of food reign supreme in your daily diet. Nutritionists have also pointed out that unless you have an allergy to gluten, there is no reason it shouldn't be part or your diet. I will state what we all know: the main focus on our daily consumption should always be a mixture of vegetables, fruits, protein, carbohydrates, and dairy. How you put this together depends on your body and your needs. I believe in the theory that if you deprive yourself of some of your "cravings," then it works to your disadvantage. Yes, it takes willpower, however, a few slices of pizza every now and then, or a wonderful chocolate mousse on a special night out, is not going to throw your training in disarray. If you are a triathlete, I already know you have determination, willpower, and a strong work ethic that you live by. Moderating your diet should not be a problem for you.

I have a handful of go-to foods for breakfast and lunch, and I do not stray too far from these items. I enjoy eating them, and I am positive that I am receiving the proper nutrition from these foods. This is not a groundbreaking diet that will be written about in health magazines because it is simple. My food choices create consistency in my diet, ease in preparation, and little anxiety when faced with a choice of dishes at a restaurant. My body is used to these items, and I stick to them in my everyday life, especially during race week. Change is never a good thing before a race, and it can disrupt the delicate balance in your system. There is little deviation from these items I can find almost anywhere, including airports. I use marinades, rubs, and condiments to change and spice up the dishes, and I am always experimenting and tweaking them to keep things interesting. The point is that the core nutrition remains the same. I eat some combination of the following daily:

Breakfast

Eggs (whole egg or egg white depending on my mood), Bungalow Munch Granola, banana, toast and Nutella or jam, breakfast burrito with egg and vegetables, chicken sausage, yogurt, waffles, pancakes, French toast, potatoes (hash browns)

Lunch

Eggs, turkey sandwich with cheese, chicken, potato chips, toast and Nutella or jam, almonds

This may not look too exciting at first glance, but the combination of these foods fuels me day to day. The dishes might be prepared differently—like having eggs over medium or huevos rancheros style—

but the core foods and nutrition do not change. My advice is to keep it simple and don't stray too much on the first two core meals of the day.

Snacks

Carrots and hummus, granola, Greek yogurt, chocolate milk, chocolate pudding, almonds, rice chips, string cheese, cheese and crackers

I snack the same way I eat my breakfast and lunch, meaning I keep it simple and usually the same items. Snacking occurs throughout the day whenever I feel slight hunger pains. I am sure you have read the theory of eating several small meals a day and how it helps metabolism. My day does not lend itself to eating several meals all day long, but I certainly adhere to what I call snacking. I must sound like a broken record, but snacking should also be done in moderation. You have to figure out how much and what your body needs during the day and then make sure you accomplish this important task.

Dinner

Salmon, tuna, chicken, sweet potatoes, turkey burgers, shrimp, crab cakes, fish, brown rice, barbeque chicken pizza, avocado, beans, quinoa

Dinner is where I allow myself to branch out and occasionally try different items. I do have certain foods that are usually in my dinner dishes so that I am sure I am obtaining the proper nutrition, but I try to be more adventurous with my selections. This is where I eat tasty appetizers, like cheesy spinach and artichoke dip, or indulge in a chocolate dessert. It is tough to maintain my focus on eating healthy at a dinner with family and friends, but I try my best and keep in mind that I kept my plan for breakfast and lunch. The items above are the majority of my staples.

From my list of items in all four genres, you can infer a few trends. Vegetables are not a huge part of my diet. I do eat them if there is an enticing side dish, if they are imbedded in a burrito, or if I order a side salad. For the most part, I might not eat vegetables on a daily basis, but I have devised a way to get the proper nutrition through vitamins and non-vegetable foods. Vegetables, I have discovered, occasionally upset my stomach. They are what I refer to as carnage because of the havoc they play on my stomach in the digestion process. I definitely do not eat any vegetables four days before a race because of the stomach "rumbling" that results.

You may also have noted I do not have too much gluten in my diet. This has been one of those trial and error things that led me to the realization I just feel better with less gluten. I also do not consume any gluten four days before a race. This takes some planning, yet it is worth it if it keeps me from having stomach issues during the race. The majority of my diet consists of a protein as the main dish and usually some sort of potato, rice, quinoa or bean as my side. I sprinkle in vegetables, nuts, dairy, and grains, though there may be days when I do not consume these items. You will be surprised how creative you can get with your proteins to keep things interesting.

The last trend you may have observed is scheduling and simplicity. I try to keep the same eating schedule no matter how "creative" my schedule gets because it is important to maintain continuity for peak performance. Most jobs have daily repetition, which helps to create a sense of order in the office. The same should hold true for your eating schedule. Develop a menu that is simple to remember and put together, and it will be one less item to stress over during your week. Repetition develops into familiarity, which leads to being able to perform without distractions. The body does not respond well to change, so avoid large deviations in your nutritional routine, especially during race week.

My nutrition suggestions are based on what I have learned over the years in developing my own diet. You can pick and choose which of my tips may fit your routine and the way your body operates. Hopefully there are some nuggets here that will help improve your overall health and performance. As I have repeatedly said, what works for me may not for you, but my goal has always been to lay the information out there and then you can decide what to do with it. I believe we all can enjoy eating healthy and through our diet see the results in our athletic endeavor.

- It is necessary to eat within thirty minutes of waking up. This stimulates your metabolism and is one of the keys to proper digestion throughout the day.
- It is an overused phrase, but right on the mark: moderation is the key to successful nutrition.

- Proper hydration is necessary for proper digestion. You should always consume liquids when you eat.
- Snacking is a key to curbing your hunger and keeping your metabolism firing properly.
- Do the research to figure out how many calories your body should consume daily, and then be smart about the food you eat to obtain these calories.
- Keep it simple. Discover nutritious foods you enjoy and make these your staples. Develop different dishes with these staples to keep things interesting.
- I do not eat vegetables and gluten four days before a race. Stomach issues have been non-existent during races since I enacted this rule (knock on wood).
- Eating well doesn't just happen. You should lay out your daily/weekly menu just like you set up your weekly training schedule.
- Do not let a disruption in your routine throw off your diet. This includes travel. Plan accordingly so you do not have an excuse for missing a meal.
- Do not confuse fueling (putting calories in your body) with nutrition. Eating gels or drinking protein shakes does not take the place of proper nutrition.

Fueling

Fueling is the last part of the dietary equation and is often the most confusing. The simple definition of fueling is what you consume during and after your workouts. It does *not* take the place of proper nutrition and it *is* necessary for maximum output during your training and appropriate recovery. Without proper fueling, your body is prone to cravings later in the day, which may result in bad decisions on the foods you consume for nutrition. There is also the false notion that not fueling will result in more calories burned, and as a consequence, you lose more weight. This actually has the opposite effect. Your metabolism slows down, and you crave more bad foods later in the day. The body, with proper fueling, is able to gain the nutrients it needs when it requires them most to promote faster recovery.

My fueling, just like my nutrition, consists of a few staples. I use them on a consistent basis, thus my body gets used to the products and there is no disruption on race day. It should be a part of your training routine, just like packing your workout gear or hydrating. I usually try to ingest 250–300 calories per hour during intense training or a race, and I get them from the products below. I also try to drink a protein shake within thirty minutes following a workout.

Fueling

Protein shake with chocolate milk, gels, blocks, protein bars, hydrating drink (coconut water, Gatorade)

My former coach, Matt Dixon did a good job of addressing nutrition, fueling, and recovery in his article "Eating for Recovery," parts of which I have included below to give you further information on these topics.

"Eating for Recovery" by Matt Dixon

"I have yet to meet a training endurance athlete who fuels enough to support their training and health needs." This was a quote I found myself saying the other day and is an appropriate start for a discussion on fueling around workouts. Nutrition and fueling for training is one of the most confusing components of endurance performance, with not only plenty of conflicting and poor information on the subject, but also plenty of data found in the labs of scientists that don't necessarily translate to the real world. To frame the subject we have to first realize that nutrition is not an isolated topic, and any successful coach or athlete will understand that it always has to be considered as a part of the overall training plan, in conjunction with the endurance training and integrated recovery. Nutrition is a supporter of your training and metabolic health, both in what you eat during and immediately following your training (your fueling), and what you eat during the rest of your day (your nutrition).

… I believe that success for endurance athletes always begins with proper fueling—those calories taken in during and immediately following training. There are four reasons I believe in proper fueling:

1. Performance During A Workout

The obvious reason is the only one most people think about, which leads many to the mistaken belief that if they can last through a three-hour bike ride with minimal calories, they must be fine!

2. Recovery

… Proper fueling maximizes recovery from any single workout, allowing readiness for the next.

3. Later Food Choices

Proper fueling, in terms of amount and type of fuel, makes positive food choices easier later in the day. These choices would focus on our building blocks (proteins), nutrients (vegetables and fruit), and good oils. Fueling well will prevent strong urges for starchy carbohydrates and sweet foods at the inappropriate time.

4. Minimizing Metabolic Stress

Our metabolic system has to deal with multiple stressors in life, as well as the massive physiological stress of our training, and inadequate fueling becomes another additional strain on the system. Proper fueling actually offsets some of the stress of training and facilitates healthy homeostasis of our metabolic health. This is a central reason for caution in carb-depletion activities pushed by some coaches.

To gain the benefits of the four points above, I urge athletes to philosophically attempt to offset any caloric deficit they have created in training within ninety minutes following activity. …Post workout, your goal is to replenish depleted stores through carbohydrate ingestion, as well as stimulate protein synthesis. This post-workout meal is the most important meal of the day for any endurance athlete. Period. Plenty of carbohydrates are valuable, but ensure you support with plenty of easily digestible protein and a little fat.

If, and only if, you follow this general path, you can then minimize starchy carbohydrates in the rest of the day; after all, your muscle glycogen stores will only get depleted in starvation and exercise. Focus instead on meats, veggies, oils, and hydration. You will repair the muscles, recover well, and be on the route to optimal performance and a leaner frame. Best of luck.

End

*

The main concept to take away from this article is that fueling is a lot different than your everyday nutrition and speeds up recovery.

Triathletes need to be proficient in three disciplines in races that can span from two to sixteen hours. Neglecting your fueling can have adverse effects on your ability to finish workouts and races. The old, outdated concept of working out and not eating to lose weight is completely false and will inevitably result in not reaching your goals. With proper nutrition and fueling, your body will thank you by its athletic performance, improved physical appearance, and overall healthiness.

Average Nutrition and Fueling

Below is an outline of my nutrition and fueling in an average week, which will give you an idea of how much a pro triathlete consumes. These are averages based on a typical training and working week where I eat at home, go out to restaurants, and fuel during workouts. I have indicated calories based on information off labels and the internet, but it is tough to be completely accurate with everything consumed. However, it is a good overview.

Monday

- Breakfast: Banana and Nutella, 300 calories; two pieces of toast, 160 calories; three scoops of granola, 375 calories
- Training: Gels and blocks, 500 calories
- Post Training: Protein shake, 400 calories
- Lunch: Turkey sandwich with pepper jack cheese and mustard, 350 calories; Baked Lays chips, 120 calories
- Snack: Carrots and hummus, 150 calories; two scoops of granola, 250 calories
- Dinner: Two turkey burgers, 500 calories; sweet potato, 180 calories; almonds, 165 calories; scoop of chocolate frozen yogurt, 225 calories
- Total: 3675 calories

Tuesday

- Breakfast: Banana and Nutella, 300 calories; two pieces of toast, 160 calories; three scoops of granola, 375 calories
- Training: Gels, 250 calories
- Post Training: Protein shake, 400 calories
- Lunch: Three eggs over easy, 270 calories; rice chips, 140 calories; toast with jelly, 120 calories

- Snack: Yogurt, 100 calories; two scoops of granola, 150 calories
- Training: Gels and blocks, 500 calories
- Dinner: One and a half grilled chicken breasts over salad, 500 calories; brown rice, 225 calories; brownie, 250 calories
- Total: 3240 calories

Wednesday

- Breakfast: Three eggs scrambled in corn tortilla, 320 calories; salsa, 36 calories; low fat cheddar cheese, 50 calories
- Training: Gels, 250 calories
- Post Training: Protein shake, 400 calories
- Lunch: Turkey panini with pepper jack cheese, 350 calories; carrots and hummus, 150 calories
- Snack: Yogurt, 100 calories; two scoops of granola, 250 calories; chocolate milk, 400 calories
- Training: Gels, 250 calories
- Dinner: Seared tuna over a salad, 350 calories; sweet potato, 180 calories; chocolate pudding, 102 calories
- Total: 3188 calories

Thursday

- Breakfast: Six egg whites, 100 calories; two pieces of toast, 160 calories; Nutella, 200 calories
- Training: Gels, 250 calories
- Post Training: Protein shake, 400 calories
- Lunch: Breakfast burrito with eggs, 400 calories; potatoes, 150 calories; low fat cheddar cheese, 50 calories; vegetables, 60 calories
- Snack: Chocolate pudding, 102 calories; rice chips, 140 calories
- Training: Gels, 500 calories
- Dinner: Two grilled chicken breasts, 530 calories; barbeque sauce, 60 calories; brown rice, 225 calories; one scoop chocolate frozen yogurt, 225 calories
- Total: 3552 calories

Friday

- Breakfast: Banana and Nutella, 300 calories; one piece of toast, 80 calories; three scoops of granola, 375 calories

- Training: Gels, 500 calories
- Post Training: Protein shake, 400 calories
- Lunch: Turkey sandwich with pepper jack cheese, 350 calories; carrots and hummus, 150 calories
- Snack: Yogurt, 100 calories; two scoops of granola, 250 calories; chocolate milk, 400 calories
- Dinner: Salmon, 300 calories; sweet potato, 180 calories; almonds, 165 calories; cheese and crackers, 195 calories
- Total: 3745 calories

Saturday

- Breakfast: Banana and Nutella, 300 calories; two pieces of toast, 160 calories; three scoops of granola, 375 calories
- Training: Gels and blocks (long outdoor ride), 1000 calories
- Post Training: Protein shake, 400 calories
- Lunch: Chicken burrito with avocado, cheese, rice, and vegetables, 710 calories
- Snack: Two scoops of granola, 250 calories; almonds, 165 calories
- Dinner: Seared tuna over a salad, 350 calories; beans and rice, 216 calories; smoked salmon and toast, 300 calories; sundae, 350 calories
- Total: 4576 calories

Sunday

- Breakfast: Banana and Nutella, 300 calories; two pieces of toast, 160 calories; yogurt, 100 calories
- Training: Gels, 250 calories
- Brunch: Huevos rancheros eggs, 400 calories; two pieces of toast with jam, 240 calories; chicken sausage, 160 calories
- Snack: Yogurt, 100 calories; two scoops of granola, 250 calories; chocolate milk, 400 calories
- Training: Gels, 250 calories
- Dinner: BBQ chicken pizza, 800 calories
- Total: 3410 calories

So, that is the average week for me. How about leading up to a race? Now, that is entirely different.

Week Before a Race

To keep a record, I wrote down everything I consumed before Ironman New Zealand 2012 (which ended up being a 70.3 race due to weather). This was a running tally in my journal of everything I ate and drank from the time I did a charity ride and then got on a plane to New Zealand to the awards banquet after the race. Even though I was in a foreign country, I was able to easily locate the food I needed for proper nutrition. In addition to consuming fluids, nutrition, and fuel, every day I took the supplements and vitamins outlined in the "Supplements and Vitamins" chapter in this manual.

Saturday

- Breakfast: Two pieces of toast; banana
- Training: Blocks while running
- Post Training: Protein shake
- Lunch: Two eggs; spinach cheese crepes
- Snack: Banana muffin
- Post-Charity Ride: protein shake
- Dinner: Grilled veggie burrito with guacamole; tortilla chips; grapes
- Snack: Half a bag of Pretzel M&M's
- Snack: Chocolate milk
- Plane to New Zealand: Plain baked potato; roll; salad
- Water throughout day and plane ride: 48 ounces; 32 ounces; 32 ounces
- Vitamin Water: 16 ounces
- Gatorade: 16 ounces

Sunday

- Plane to New Zealand continued: Fruit cup; two rice cakes with peanut butter; banana
- Snack: Applesauce
- Snack: Gluten-free cookie
- Snack: Small hot chocolate
- Lunch: Scrambled eggs; two small hash browns; two pieces of toast
- Snack: Gluten-free cookie

- Snack: Toast and one ounce jelly
- Snack: Rice chips and hummus
- Dinner: Shrimp; one and a half cups of jasmine rice; vegetables
- Snack: Reese's Dark Chocolate Peanut Butter Cup
- Water throughout day: 16 ounces; 48 ounces; 16 ounces
- Gatorade: 16 ounces
- Powerade: 16 ounces

Monday

- Breakfast: Banana; bowl of cereal with nonfat milk
- Snack: Slice of toast with Nutella
- Training: Half of a lolly cake (during swim)
- Training: Blocks, one pack
- Post Training: Protein bar
- Snack: Hot chocolate
- Lunch: Eggs scrambled; two pieces toast with honey
- Snack: Banana; jam; half cup of trail mix
- Snack: Rice chips and hummus
- Dinner: Salmon, six ounces; four mini new potatoes; vegetable stack; salad
- Snack: Reese's Dark Chocolate Peanut Butter Cup
- Water throughout day: 16 ounces; 48 ounces; 16 ounces
- Gatorade: 32 ounces
- Sparkling water: 16 ounces

Tuesday

- Breakfast: Banana; two pieces toast with peanut butter and Nutella
- Snack: Bowl of cereal with nonfat milk
- Training: Blocks, one pack
- Post Training: Luna protein bar (after ride)
- Snack: Hot chocolate
- Lunch: Scrambled eggs; toast with jam; hash browns
- Snack: Gluten-free pretzels with hummus
- Snack: Two skewers of chicken satay with peanut sauce

- Dinner: Shrimp stir fry with jasmine rice
- Snack: Half a cup of trail mix
- Snack: Reese's Dark Chocolate Peanut Butter Cup
- Water throughout day: 48 ounces; 16 ounces
- Hydrating drink with electrolytes: 24 ounces
- Gatorade: 32 ounces
- Sparkling water: 16 ounces

Wednesday
- Breakfast: Banana and bowl of cereal with nonfat milk
- Training: Protein bar
- Post Training: Protein shake
- Lunch: Scrambled eggs; two bananas; gluten-free toast; clementine
- Snack: Half a cup of trail mix
- Dinner: Rice pilaf; three skewers of chicken satay
- Snack: Reese's Dark Chocolate Peanut Butter Cup; toast with Nutella
- Water throughout day: 30 ounces
- Hydrating drink with electrolytes: 40 ounces
- Gatorade: 64 ounces

Thursday
- Breakfast: Banana; one bowl of cereal with nonfat milk; gluten-free toast with Nutella
- Post Training: Protein bar
- Lunch: Scrambled eggs; gluten-free toast with jam; hash browns
- Snack: Protein shake
- Snack: Gluten-free pretzels
- Snack: Gluten-free lemon square
- Dinner: Grilled chicken: boiled potatoes; two pieces cheese pizza
- Snack: One-quarter Snickers bar; one-quarter 3 Musketeers bar
- Water throughout day: 40 ounces; 16 ounces; 24 ounces

- Sparkling water: 16 ounces
- Gatorade: 48 ounces

Friday

- Breakfast: Banana; gluten-free protein bar
- Lunch: Scrambled eggs; two pieces of gluten-free toast; hot chocolate; sliced banana; dark chocolate
- Snack: Two pieces of gluten-free toast with Nutella
- Snack: Luna protein bar
- Snack: Gluten-free pretzels
- Dinner: Chicken; rice; egg
- Snack: Two skewers chicken satay
- Snack: One-quarter Snickers bar
- Water throughout day: 32 ounces; 48 ounces; 48 ounces
- Hydrating drink with electrolytes: 12 ounces
- Gatorade: 24 ounces

Saturday, Race day—70.3 distance
Pre Race:

- Water: 24 ounces
- Breakfast: Two pieces of toast with Nutella; banana
- Protein shake
- Pre Swim: three blocks
- *During Race:*
- Bike: Blocks, two and a half packs during fifty-six miles
- Bike: Hydrating drink with electrolytes, three 16 ounce bottles, 200 calories per bottle
- Bike: Two tabs electrolytes
- Run, mile one: Gel, vanilla
- Run, mile four: Gel, double espresso
- Run, mile eight: Gel, vanilla
- Run: Water and Red Bull, sips throughout run
Post Race:
- McDonald's large fries; two pieces cheese pizza
- Awards banquet: Roll with butter; salad

As you can see, there are some notable omissions from my race-week intake that I consume during an average week, but the general direction of my nutrition and fueling is the same. My intake of gluten and vegetables was reduced throughout the week and I had very little of either four days before the race. From my journal, I can tell that I was not hydrating enough, although I did average roughly 130–160 ounces of liquid per day throughout the week. Eggs constituted a lot of my diet, in addition to chicken and bananas. These items are my staples for obtaining a lot of the nutrition I need for the race. My carbohydrates consisted of potatoes and rice, but these were consumed in what I consider normal portions; I did not carbohydrate load because it is not necessary. The energy for race-day performance comes from fueling immediately before and during the event. I will break my race-day nutrition down in more detail in the "Race Week" chapter, but the race-day nutrition above is a broad overview to show that fueling is the bread and butter of performance.

Recovery

The last concept I want to touch on is recovery. It is the time necessary for the repair of damage to the body and mind brought about by training or competition. People ask me how I have completed over fifty Ironman events, or how I can race so much during the course of a year without sacrificing results. First of all, I really like to race. Nothing beats the anticipation during race week of the upcoming event, followed by the competition of race day with so many amazing athletes all pushing toward the same goal. There is no secret formula to being able to race on a consistent basis; it just takes discipline to complete the post-race tasks we all know how to do but consistently neglect (myself included).

An athlete needs rest after a race—lots of it. This is the best recovery tool known, and there is no substitute for it. If you do not get copious amounts of sleep after a race, the time needed to fully recover increases and you run the risk toeing the line of your next event in less than peak condition. Rest was something I severely lacked as an age group athlete because I had to go to work on the Monday after a race and sit for ten hours behind a desk. This is not a winning formula for my next race, but it was a necessity because I had to earn a paycheck. The company did not care that I just completed a ten-hour race the prior day. As a pro triathlete, sleep is part of my business and is scheduled accordingly. If I do not get proper rest, my body may not be in racing shape and my business suffers. I try to stay off my feet and use Recovery Boots, use Vector450 and ice as much as possible five days following a race. I try to sleep whenever the urge hits me. This is not a luxury I could afford as an age-grouper, but it is a necessity in my current situation.

Even though I love racing, it is a business for me, and I have to treat it like a day at the office. Apple does not shut its doors for two days after a big announcement about the new iPad; it is business as usual, and the company keeps on humming. There is no downtime to relish in your achievements after a race. You need to immediately focus on your next race because the five days after an event are crucial to your recovery and development. This includes keeping on your nutritional schedule. You should not shut this down immediately after a race; the temptation to splurge and eat junk food is strong because you want to "treat" yourself, but rein that feeling in. After a race is one of the most important times to eat correctly so your body can absorb the proper nutrients to aid in rebuilding the cells and muscles. You can indulge a little to keep yourself sane, but if you have another race in the near future, keep your eyes on the prize and don't divert from proper nutrition.

You should attempt to get back into training as soon as possible. However, be smart about it. I try to get my blood flowing the day after a race, even after a ten-hour Ironman, to loosen the muscles and help clear out the lactic acid build up. I usually gingerly swim in the pool for forty-five minutes and slowly build from there for the next five days. It is important to rest your muscles, but you don't want them to lie dormant for a week. Going from doing nothing to your normal training schedule could possibly lead to injury and delay your development into your next event. This is a metamorphous period where your body deals with the traumatic stress you just put it through and rebuilds. As you train your body to deal with the stress and recover properly, it makes it easier to come back quicker to your normally functioning self. Remember, the body is resilient and has to be trained to recover just like it trains for performance. Create the post-race foundation for a helpful environment for this regeneration.

Conclusion

Remember to use these tips on hydration, nutrition, fueling, and recovery as a guide but not *your* exact protocol. You have to figure out most of this on your own, since everyone's body is different and nutritional needs are never exactly the same. There is no cookie cutter approach I can offer that everyone can use. Apply my suggestions to your particular needs with the tweaks to fit your body. One hundred and eighty pound Chris Lieto, who completes an Ironman a lot faster than I do, would starve using my nutrition as his guide. Most triathletes, including myself, would find the liquid I consume inadequate, which is why I keep journals to chart my intake. I am continually looking for ways to improve my hydration and overall racing. The consumption levels for hydration, nutrition, and fueling will come with practice, experimentation, and time. Knowing and sticking with your adequate hydration, nutrition, and fueling, combined with a structured recovery routine, will help you reach that equilibrium in less time than you would without the proper foundation in place.

SUPPLEMENTS AND VITAMINS

Navigating the world of supplements and vitamins is an intimidating task. Some athletes swear by their own magical formula that they use during a regular training week and around race time. Others are still trying to find the elusive combination that will help their bodies perform and then easily recover. Athletes also face the problem of recognizing what is legal and what is not, a much more overwhelming task than one may initially suspect. For example, a form of Claritin, Claritin-D, is a banned substance and can get an athlete suspended from racing. This problem is compounded when combined with the inexact science of ingesting multiple substances; the amount of information available on the countless number of supplements can be overwhelming and confusing to athletes seeking to improve their race-day performances.

I guess the one thing everyone can agree on is that supplements, if taken with the oversight of a doctor and with a careful eye on the banned substance list, can help your body both physically and mentally. The physical benefits are the ones most discussed because not all nutrition can be absorbed from the food you eat. Lack of nutrients, combined with the tremendous strain under which triathletes put their bodies, is a recipe for fatigue and physical breakdown.

The mental aspect of supplements, however, is the one I find most intriguing. Knowing they are supplying their body with additional health benefits can boost athletes' confidence, which results in performance improvements. I have often felt the supplements I take are, in fact, a placebo passing through my body with no added value. Nevertheless, they have become a part of my routine, and it benefits me mentally to know I am bolstering my body with additional supplements, placebo or not.

Professional male triathlete TJ Tollakson posed a supplement-related question on Twitter on February 13, 2012, and received over twenty-five different answers in less than three hours. Below was his question and I snipped a few of the answers to give you an idea of the plethora of products on the market.

Twitter Feed:

From TJ Tollakson:
What's your must have list of supplements for health and/or performance include? I use HMB, Beta Alanine, CoQ10, Omega3, astaxanthin - @tollakson on Twitter
Replies:

- <name> N-acetylcystiene 900mg 2x a day. Puts other antioxidants to shame.
- 3 hours ago - <name> BASE Performance Supplements!
- 2 hours ago - <name> Zinc, B12, Megadoses -Vit C, a little Maca every now and then.
- 2 hours ago - <name> NAC 900mg 2x daily with EmergenC (courtesy of my fav Tucson based chiro <name>;), Beta Alanine, Cordygen 5, Omega 3, multivit. On the beta Alanine, I take 2000mg pre workout, another 2000mg post workout and another 2000mg end of day.
- about an hour ago - <name> Omega 3 (Krill oil), Astaxanthin, BCAAs, Alpha-Lipoic Acid, and Alpha Ketoglutarate on Race day
- about an hour ago - <name> D-Ribose (5g), Cordyceps, Medium chain triglycerides, R-ALA (not ALA), Evodiamine, 3% Rosavins, Vinpocetine and Hyperzine A.
- about an hour ago - <name> Beta Alanine is good, but a fad ingredient. 6,000 mg a day is way over kill to buffer lactic acid, which will prevent the true effect of ammonia depletion.

It is difficult to dissect which supplements and vitamins to take, because as we have seen with TJ's post, everyone has an opinion, and there is no right answer. TJ is one of the smartest racers on the circuit and is constantly looking for ways to gain a competitive advantage. Periodically polling what others are using is a brilliant way to discover new products. The problem is everyone's body reacts differently to supplements, and the only way to discover what works is through trial and error. The other X factor is how your mind will react to these supplements. I have stopped taking pills because they were too big, or after having a bad training week, I blamed the vitamin specifically. In reality, the pill probably had nothing to do with my performance, but if my mind is not confident in the product, it will ultimately affect my racing.

The supplements I take now are the result of years of experimentation and talking with doctors, nutritionists, coaches, and pro triathletes. I try to keep it simple so I am not a walking biochemistry experiment, and I have reduced my total intake to five to ten different pills per day, depending on the time of the month and if there is a race approaching. I have experimented with many of the products mentioned in TJ's Twitter feed with mixed results. Beta-alanine is a supplement that comes to mind where individuals in the tri community preach its benefits, yet I did not have positive results when I used it. I could have been in a rut with my training, or it just did not add anything to my workouts. Regardless, my experimentation was brief, and I ruled it out of my program. The choice comes down to what works for you, what you believe in, and what your doctor or nutritionist recommends.

You should consult with a professional concerning your supplement and vitamin intake, or the consequences could be dire. When you are dealing with pushing your body to the limits during a two- to sixteen-hour triathlon, any decision relating to what you are ingesting, could result in death. Thus, it is imperative to tell your doctor everything you are taking, whether it is triathlon related or not, so you can get professional medical approval before proceeding with your regimen. The minor annoyance of receiving a diagnosis you are not happy with from your doctor far outweighs the potential dangers associated with mixing medication and supplements.

I cannot stress enough the importance of getting professional approval for your food, vitamin, and supplement intake. I have personally had a few experiences where the wrong combination was disastrous, and in extreme circumstances, could have been fatal. Sodium citrate is a product used by triathletes in preparation for a hot, long race day. It is in a variety of the endurance drinks on the market. I had collapsed at mile twenty-two in St. George in 2011 from dehydration and lack of electrolytes. My kidneys have always been in a weakened state because of my problems with dehydration, and passing out on a hot day did not improve my condition. I was told by a trusted source to load sodium citrate before my next Ironman to help combat the hydration problems I have had my entire racing career. I did not consult a doctor and proceeded to follow this advice.

My first major error was accepting an opinion without doing my own research. The second error was that I did this right before an important race with zero practice beforehand. The third error was I did not consult a doctor. These three major mistakes resulted in my pulling out of the race at mile seventy on the bike after I gained fifteen pounds of water weight, could barely see, and felt light headed; this was not a good combination on a bike. I learned later, after thinking it was an allergic reaction to a bee sting or pollen and being treated for this, that my kidneys were not functioning, and it was a potentially fatal situation. The wrong supplement, combined with weak kidneys and an inaccurate diagnosis and medical treatment, resulted in another long hospital stay and being bedridden for four days. I was in good shape before I changed my racing menu. Ultimately, I discovered the new combination was not only bad for my system, but it could have been lethal.

I am listing below what I take supplement-wise to give you an example of what *one* pro does to prepare herself for everyday training and racing. This is **not** something you should copy item for item, because a substance I use could have an adverse effect on your bodily systems. This *does* show that you do not have to use every hot new product on the market to be an effective triathlete. Remember, supplements are used to *complement* the nutrients you should be receiving from the food you eat. As triathletes, we expend so much energy through training and our life-styles that it is extremely difficult to obtain all we need from the foods we eat. It is not impossible but definitely hard to do. I use products that will add to the vitamins I am lacking in my current diet— ones that help me recover, help ward off illness, and effectively mute some of the pain and discomfort of the female menstrual cycle. My intent is to offer my thoughts on what is available and my reasons for using the product. Once again, **this is not a doctor's opinion on each supplement**; it is purely what I hope to gain from the product. The dosages I outline are from the specific brands I buy. **Do not use them as an exact guide, and you should consult your doctor before using any vitamins**. There is a vast world of products designed to help keep your performance and your body in top shape, protecting you from the rigors of athletics combined with a hectic life. Below, I have divided the supplements, vitamins, and medication into seven separate categories based on the activity and time of month.

Daily

Calcium, 350 mg

All athletes can use some calcium in their diets to strengthen bones and to help heal breaks. It is no secret triathletes have a high risk for bike accidents, so it is precautionary to take calcium to try to prevent a break. I increased my dosage when I broke my back after a bike accident in August of 2012. However, in the age of more is better, be careful not to take too much calcium because it can lead to kidney stones and other health issues. You should monitor what you are receiving from the foods you eat, like yogurt and milk, before deciding to take additional calcium.

CM Plex, 700 mg

This natural product aids in the hydration of joints. When I was an amateur, I routinely had achy joints, which impeded my training and caused major discomfort at night. I was on the path to arthritis in my forties. I found CM Plex because my mother-in-law worked for Unicity, a company that developed their own cutting-edge, natural vitamins and products. I started taking it on her recommendation with outstanding results. The pain subsided, and I had more mobility in my joints.

Enzygen Plus, 464 mg

This is another Unicity product, and it aids in digestion. There are few triathletes who have not had stomach problems while training or on race day; it is a side effect of a sport where you push your body to its limits. Any product that can help breakdown fats, carbohydrates, and protein to try to prevent stomach calamities is worth researching and using.

Glucosamine Chondroitin, 950 mg
There have been many studies done on this product. Some individuals believe it works with joint health, while others are skeptical. I am a big believer because the combination of CM Plex and Glucosamine has greatly reduced my joint discomfort, which is important in the sport of triathlon.

Iron/Slow FE, 28 mg
Iron helps in transporting oxygen to your body's cells, including your muscles, and you can usually obtain your daily allowance through the food you eat. However, deficiency leads to fatigue, general body weakness, and deficiency-related health ailments. Iron has a myriad of benefits that are a must for this triathlete.

Vitamin D, 1000 IU
A vitamin D supplement was recommended to me to aid with healthy bone density and immunity. For females in particular, calcium and vitamin D are important to maintain a healthy skeleton. You should be able to synthesize some vitamin D from the sun, but, as we all know, overexposure is not healthy for your skin, and it is also tough to obtain sufficient sun exposure in the winter months.

Pre Period—Two Weeks Before
Aspirin, 81 mg
One of the benefits of aspirin is it does help with alleviating the discomfort associated with menstrual symptoms. This is a low dosage preparation two weeks before the period to have it running through my system to help minimize the effects.

Magnesium, 400 mg
This substance helps with menstrual cramps and PMS. When I researched magnesium, I found the main effect it has on cramps is as a muscle relaxant, which reduces the contractions of the uterus.

Omega-3, 1000 mg
I am sure you have heard of this trendy supplement that has shown to

have many long-lasting benefits from increasing memory to lowering blood pressure. You can absorb these fatty acids from fish, the most popular being salmon, which I eat on a regular basis. It is believed that omega-3 can reduce inflammation and pain during your period.

Pre Period—One Week Before

Ibuprofen, 200 mg

Most of us know ibuprofen is an anti-inflammatory product; I have found it also helps with cramping. A majority of triathletes use ibuprofen for an array of ailments. Some women also claim it helps them with menstrual fatigue, which certainly works against you at race time. Please note excessive use of ibuprofen leading up to and before a race can lead to health problems. If you already have weak kidneys and race on a hot day while consuming the product, this combination can lead to a potentially devastating dehydration problem. I was using four to six tablets of ibuprofen a day four weeks leading up to an important race to help with the pain after my bike crash. I came into the race dehydrated because of this usage, and the hot temperatures only added to the dire situation. I ended up feeling the effects halfway through the bike and never recovered during that race. **Please do your research and consult a doctor before using ibuprofen.** It silently derailed me in an important race, and the damage could have been worse.

One Week Before a Race

Aspirin, 81 mg

In additional to alleviating menstrual discomfort, aspirin is known to help with blood flow throughout your body. Combined with compression socks, Aspirin should allow constant blood flow in your limbs, where a triathlete needs it most.

Quecertin with Bromelain, 250 mg (Quecertin); 125 mg (Bromelain)

Research shows this is a powerful antioxidant and has anti-inflammatory capabilities. It is crucial a week before a race when the last thing you want is to get sick. Inflammation can lead to a host of diseases, which is why your body tries to control it. Quecertin with Bromelain aids in this fight.

Selenium, 0.2 mg or 200 mcg

This is a mineral that has antioxidant properties, which protect cells from damage and thus, help deter disease. You want to arrive at the starting line of your race in peak condition, and this substance helps the body achieve this state.

Flying to a Race
Aspirin, 81 mg

There are many documented benefits to aspirin, but I use it before flying to reduce the risk of blood clots. I also wear compression socks and tights on the plane. For longer flights, I may take two 81 mg pills of aspirin because sitting in one position for so long restricts the blood flow, which increases the risk for clots, even in healthy athletes. Of course, there are also leg exercises you can do on the plane that are supposed to help keep blood clots at bay.

Vitamin C, 1000 mg

The airplane is a germ tube; prepare by taking vitamin C before flying to an event to help fend off illness. Travel is stressful and can weaken the body, and it is important to take the proper steps to keep the body healthy in an unhealthy atmosphere. Please note that vitamin C has a diuretic effect on the body, so it is important to stay hydrated. Additionally, large amounts of vitamin C can upset your stomach. I was coming down with a cold at Ironman Arizona in 2011, and I overloaded on vitamin C two days prior to the race and on race day. The result was that I visited the bathroom quite often on the run because too much of the vitamin caused diarrhea. Lesson learned.

Race Day
BASE Electrolyte Salt

I use the BASE Performance product BASE Electrolyte Salt because it has multiple components, but it does not contain sodium citrate, which my body does not handle well. I broke my own rule, never to try something new on race day, and took it during Ironman Arizona in 2014 during the race after a recommendation from founder Chris Lieto. I have used it ever since and trust the direction of owners Matt Miller and Tony Demakis. Depending on the heat of the race and how much water I am losing, I will decide during the race day how BASE Salt to take. I carry vials with me on the bike and run. I also try to take small amounts with my meals a few days before the race to get my body used to them.

Imodium A-D / TUMS

As a new pro, an experienced pro male triathlete gave me a tip about my stomach problems on the run. He mentioned he always ate two TUMS tablets before the run. This seemed to settle his stomach so he was not constantly running to the bathroom on the course. I practiced this in my bike to run training and used them one race, and it did the trick. I have since adjusted my diet so I no longer have stomach issues, but I still carry a few TUMS with me, just in case.

Post-Race Recovery

Vitamin B-Complex, 1550 mg

I use the B-Complex 100 product from Vitamin Shoppe, which contains numerous ingredients (vitamins B_1, B_2, B_3, B_6, etc.) to comprise the 1550 mg. It is an anti-stress composition of vitamins, meaning it helps the body with everyday functions, which is advantageous after a taxing day on the racecourse. It helps break down food into energy and aids in digestion.

Melatonin, 3 mg

It seems logical that your body would crave sleep after a triathlon, yet I have found the opposite is true. I may pass out from pure exhaustion and sleep for a while, but then I awake in a couple of hours and start returning emails because I cannot fall asleep again. Your body is traumatized, and your adrenaline is still pumping, especially after an Ironman. It is confused about whether or not it should rest. Melatonin is a natural sleep aid, and I take it right before I am going to bed after a race. It does not require a large dosage to help with sleep, and I have found taking too much negates the effects.

Vitamin C, 1000 mg

The body is very susceptible to disease immediately following a race because of the trauma it has been through. It is necessary to help fight off sickness by keeping Vitamin C flowing through the body. I usually add more vitamin C than 1000 mg because it does pass through quickly with all the water I drink to replenish fluids.

Zinc, 50 mg

After an athletic event where you have pushed to your limits and beyond, your body does not have the strength to fend off disease on its own. Zinc is known to have immune boosting properties, which can help when you are extremely vulnerable after a race.

My secret to taking these different pills is a simple thirty-day pillbox to store my daily allocations. This saves me from having to keep pulling the products from their individual containers every day. If you are like a lot of Type A triathletes and do the proper research to determine the ideal times to take your supplements, you will need to purchase a seven-day pillbox with separate sections for the time of day. I have a simple system where I put masking tape on the cover of the container that marks an important day in the month. For instance, I make sure I indicate race days, one and two weeks before races, one and two weeks before my period, and travel days. I can then meticulously fill out the containers at the beginning of each month with the corresponding pills for the approaching events. I have a seven-day pill case I use when I travel and transfer the appropriate pills for easy carrying. It is never smart to change your routine going into a race, so your supplements should not be forgotten.

Usually, I take the pills after my morning workout, because the mishmash of them sloshing around during intense training tends to upset my stomach. Supplements might not be possible for individuals with sensitive stomachs that get upset with the slightest change. I have a hard time swallowing a handful of pills, so I take them one at a time with water or a post-workout protein shake. The large horse pills are a pain for me to swallow, so I tend to avoid them. I would rather take multiple smaller pills to receive the proper dosage. Most of the products I mentioned can be found at VitaminShoppe or Amazon and I also order some at Unicity.

Directions are on each bottle, noting when to ingest (before or after meals) and the recommended dosage. There is science behind all of these instructions, but you should still consult your doctor and research the product online to determine the best time to take the pill. To be frank, I am just happy to get them in my body. I have a hard enough time remembering to take the pills once a day, let alone figuring out when to take each one at different times over the course of the day. As long as they get in my body, I feel I have done my job and can go about my business. It puts my mind at ease that I am trying to give my body the proper nutrients—maybe not during the ideal times, but nonetheless, there is some absorption as they pass through my body.

The next time you overhear a conversation about the latest and greatest athletic performance supplement, do not immediately go out and purchase it. Perform your own research, consult your doctor, and talk to others who have experience with the product, and then make your own decision. I recently saw a Tweet by 70.3 specialist Angela Naeth concerning a juice product that helps her with endurance. Endorsements of a product from an athlete as talented as Angela are quite enticing, but follow the guidelines above before diving in headfirst and trying the juice. One of the triathlon golden rules is to never use a product for the first time before a race and without testing it multiple times in training. If you follow the proper procedures and like how the product makes you feel, you can be confident you have taken the steps to improve your performance. Angela's secret endurance juice can now be your gain.

It is difficult to see direct results from supplements, which is the reason so many triathletes exclude them from their daily routine. They are like preventive medicine; what you are taking now could help save your life ten years down the road. In our immediate-satisfaction society, if something is not helping us right away, we tend to drop it from our routines. Accordingly, just like the multivitamin is supposed to help the average human live longer, or heart medication is supposed to help rid arteries of plaque and prevent heart attacks, supplements should subtlety maintain a healthy body over time. The results might not be immediate or even seen but do not discount their value. The possibility of misuse is always present, but the benefits for your body, or just "in your head," may put you in a better place on race day.

THE "AVERAGE" WEEK

From the beginning, I have looked at this book as a way to answer your questions. More specifically, I have equated it, in my mind, to an interview. In a corporate job interview two common questions are, "What is your 'average' day like? What do you do for your business during the course of a week if everything goes according to plan?" Being a pro triathlete is my "nine to five" job, and I work for Meredith Kessler, Inc. I am trying to make a living, just like the Apple employee who punches the clock every day to earn a paycheck. I generate income in a different and more erratic way, but the focus is the same.

As I mentioned before, a week in my off-season looks similar to my race season because I strive for a balanced life-style to try to avoid the peaks and valleys in training. Although I set my own hours, if I do not complete my tasks, my corporation falters and I receive a reduced paycheck, if I receive any pay at all. Macro concepts of my training in an average week are diagramed in the "Training" chapter; this section focuses on the everyday details. You will see many tasks that could be labeled mundane, yet a lot of "regular" jobs have their menial tasks that have to be accomplished in order to be successful.

Bear in mind that by no means does every week go as smoothly as the one outlined below. Life is always throwing curveballs your way, just like the hiccups that can occur at a job in the corporate world. Adversity can pop up at any time; all you can do is try to maintain your schedule while you dodge bullets throughout the week.

Monday

- 6:30 a.m.–6:45 a.m. Fueling breakfast, typically two waffles, banana with Nutella, and water
- 7:00 a.m.–9:00 a.m. Indoor cycling workout; gels during and after workout
- 9:15 a.m.–9:45 a.m. Run workout off of the bike, outside

- 10:00 a.m.–11:15 a.m. Swim workout
- 11:30 a.m.–12:15 p.m. Lunch and coffee with friends
- 12:30 p.m.–1:00 p.m. Grocery store (this is part of the job to obtain the proper nutrition)
- 1:30 p.m.–2:30 p.m. Return morning emails and correspondence; Protein recovery shake mixed with chocolate milk
- 2:30 p.m.–4:30 p.m. Finish athlete coaching plans
- 4:30 p.m.–5:30 p.m. Scheduled athlete coaching calls
- 5:30 p.m.–7:00 p.m. Business-related tasks, including sponsor requests, bike maintenance, interview questions, fan emails, and blog updates
- 7:15 p.m.–8:00 p.m. Dinner with husband
- 8:15 p.m.–9:00 p.m. Maintain relationships with family and friends
- 9:00 p.m.–11:00 p.m. Work on business; use Recovery Boots or ice
- 11:00 p.m.–12:00 a.m. Prepare for next day; pack workout gear, nutrition, and hydration
- 12:00 a.m.–4:30 a.m. Sleep

Tuesday

- 4:30 a.m.–4:45 a.m. Fueling breakfast, typically two waffles, banana with Nutella, and water
- 5:00 a.m.–7:00 a.m. Group swim at local pool
- 7:15 a.m.–8:15 a.m. Interval run on treadmill or track
- 8:30 a.m.–9:00 a.m. Protein recovery shake mixed with chocolate milk
- 9:00 a.m.–11:30 a.m. Catch up on morning emails (business, sponsor, and personal)
- 11:30 a.m.–12:00 p.m. Lunch
- 12:00 p.m.–2:00 p.m. Rest; try to nap
- 2:00 p.m.–4:30 p.m. Work on business; prepare for teaching cycling class
- 5:00 p.m.–7:00 p.m. Teach indoor cycling class
- 7:00 p.m.–7:20 p.m. Short run off bike after teaching class
- 7:20 p.m.–7:40 p.m. TRX workouts
- 8:00 p.m.–10:00 p.m. Scheduled dinner with friends

- 10:00 p.m.–11:30 p.m. Recovery Boots; return emails; relax in front of TV
- 11:30 p.m.–12:00 a.m. Prepare for next day; pack workout gear, nutrition, and hydration
- 12:00 a.m.–6:30 a.m. Sleep

Wednesday

- 6:30 a.m.–6:45 a.m. Fueling breakfast, typically two waffles, banana with Nutella, and water
- 7:00 a.m.–8:30 a.m. Indoor cycling workout; gels during and after workout
- 8:45 a.m.–10:00 a.m. Indoor cycling workout; gels during and after workout
- 10:00 a.m.–10:30 a.m. Run workout off of the bike, outside
- 10:45 a.m.–11:45 a.m. Swim workout
- 12:00 p.m.–12:30 p.m. Lunch and coffee with friends
- 12:45 p.m.–3:45 p.m. Return morning emails and update athlete coaching plans
- 4:00 p.m.–4:45 p.m. Treadmill run
- 5:00 p.m.–7:00 p.m. Rest; try to nap or work on business
- 7:15 p.m.–8:00 p.m. Dinner with husband
- 8:00 p.m.–10:00 p.m. Recovery Boots or ice; catch up on emails; social media
- 10:00 p.m.–11:00 p.m. Prepare for next day; pack workout gear, nutrition, and hydration
- 11:00 p.m.–9:00 a.m. Sleep; try to sleep in as much as possible

Thursday

- 9:00 a.m.–9:15 a.m. Fueling breakfast, typically two waffles, banana with Nutella, and water
- 9:30 a.m.–11:00 a.m. Swim workout
- 11:30 a.m.–12:00 p.m. Lunch; protein recovery shake mixed with chocolate milk
- 12:15 p.m.–2:00 p.m. Return morning emails; work on business
- 2:15 p.m.–3:30 p.m. Long treadmill workout
- 3:45 p.m.–4:30 p.m. Work on business; prepare for indoor cycling class

- 5:00 p.m.–7:00 p.m. Teach indoor cycling class
- 7:00 p.m.–7:30 p.m. TRX workouts
- 8:00 p.m.–10:00 p.m. Scheduled dinner with friends
- 10:15 p.m.–11:30 p.m. Recovery Boots; return emails; relax in front of TV
- 11:30 p.m.–12:00 a.m. Prepare for next day; pack workout gear, nutrition, and hydration
- 12:00 a.m.–4:30 a.m. Sleep

Friday

- 4:30 a.m.–4:45 a.m. Fueling breakfast, typically two waffles, banana with Nutella, and water
- 5:00 a.m.–6:45 a.m. Group swim at local pool
- 7:00 a.m.–9:00 a.m. Indoor cycling workout; gels during and after workout
- 9:00 a.m.–9:30 a.m. Run workout off of the bike outside
- 10:00 a.m.–11:00 a.m. Grocery store
- 11:15 a.m.–12:00 p.m. Return morning emails; protein recovery shake mixed with chocolate milk
- 12:00 p.m.–12:30 p.m. Lunch
- 12:45 p.m.–2:00 p.m. Bike maintenance for Saturday ride: build wheels with tubular tires, charge Di2 and PowerTap computer, attach water bottle holders, and clean bike
- 2:00 p.m.–3:15 p.m. Massage
- 3:30 p.m.–5:30 p.m. Rest; try to nap
- 5:30 p.m.–7:00 p.m. Business-related tasks, including sponsor requests, interview questions, fan emails, and blog updates
- 7:00 p.m.–8:00 p.m. Dinner (usually salmon with Aaron's secret marinade—one secret I convinced him to let me share later in the book!)
- 8:00 p.m.–11:00 p.m. Recovery Boots or ice; watch a movie
- 11:00 p.m.–11:30 p.m. Prepare for next day; pack workout gear, nutrition, and hydration
- 11:30 p.m.–7:00 a.m. Sleep

Saturday

- 7:00 a.m.–7:15 a.m. Fueling breakfast, typically two waffles, banana with Nutella, and water

- 8:00 a.m.–1:00 p.m. Long ride outside; gels during and after workout
- 1:00 p.m.–2:00 p.m. Run workout off of the bike
- 2:15 p.m.–2:45 p.m. Lunch; protein recovery shake mixed with chocolate milk
- 3:00 p.m.–12:00 a.m. Family and friend's time
- 12:00 a.m.–9:00 a.m. Sleep; try to sleep in as much as possible

Sunday

- 9:00 a.m.–9:15 a.m. Fueling breakfast, typically two waffles, banana with Nutella, and water
- 9:30 a.m.–11:00 a.m. Treadmill workout or long run outside
- 11:00 a.m.–12:30 p.m. Swim workout
- 12:30 p.m.–1:00 p.m. Protein recovery shake mixed with chocolate milk
- 1:00 p.m.–2:00 p.m. Brunch with husband
- 2:15 p.m.–5:00 p.m. Athlete coaching plans for next week
- 5:00 p.m.–7:00 p.m. Plan out "things to do" for next week; return emails
- 7:15 p.m.–8:00 p.m. Dinner with husband
- 8:00 p.m.–12:00 a.m. Recovery Boots; catch up with family and friends on the phone; close emails out for the day
- 12:00 a.m.–6:30 a.m. Sleep

As you can see, the life of a pro triathlete is not glamorous—far from it. Because *you* are your business, seven-day workweeks are normal and expected to make sure you have an optimal product to showcase to the public on race day. I have found I spend more time on the computer now than I did when I worked sixty hours a week at an investment bank. Although I have more flexibility in my schedule, I still have to complete my daily tasks or my nutrition, hydration, fitness, or business will falter. The days when I used to be able to come home from the office, put up my feet, and relax for a few hours before bedtime are long gone. Now, the common scene at our home in the evenings is my husband and me on the couch, buried in our computer screens, occasionally looking up at the TV to catch the show on in the background. I sit in my pajamas, with my Recovery Boots on, trying to lighten the load of emails from the day.

Although my schedule is hectic, I always find time to spend with my husband, family, and friends, because it is very important to me to lead a balanced life. As an amateur, I also strived for balance; the difference was then I had to be at an office for ten hours a day and available on my Blackberry in the evenings. Now I follow a similar routine. I try to workout in the morning, accomplish business-related activities during the day, squeeze in another workout, make time for an extracurricular activity like a dinner with friends, and then catch up on email at night. The main change in my life is I gained flexibility; now, I typically do not need to be somewhere at a certain time. I have the opportunity to rest if my body is worn down and the ability to focus on my nutrition and hydration.

As with anything that seems difficult in life, it takes discipline to achieve a balanced schedule while training all year long. You have to know where your time is allocated in order to improve your efficiency. As I state throughout this manual, time is an extremely valuable commodity, just like your skills, earning abilities, and talents so take the effort to care for and nurture it. In my business manual, I detail suggestions on how you can make your life more efficient and free up time to do some of the things you may think are out of reach. You can begin now by creating your own weekly calendar to figure out where you are spending the majority of your time. Then, take steps to eliminate the pain points in order to free up hours for what you truly want to do with that precious commodity. If you do not know where the problems lie within your week, you cannot take the necessary steps to fix them.

Use this as a guide to point you in the right direction to create a balanced schedule. However, the reality is that people are all dealing with their own sets of personal issues—including raising children, working longer than normal work hours, coping with illness, handling relationship drama, etc. My workweek has evolved for more than ten years, as I figured out the correct balance of my priorities—training, business, family, and friends. Through it all, try to stick to your schedule and reduce your pain points, and the rest will be more manageable.

Even if you already know several of the points in these manuals, you will not know this next tidbit. I managed to coerce Aaron into telling you one of the best triathlon tips you will ever receive: the recipe for Aaron's secret salmon marinade. Guard this with ferocity. Once other athletes get wind of it, they will be enjoying this protein and omega-3 bomb with regularity. Aaron created this marinade himself through years of experimentation. This recipe is the backbone of my diet and is well worth the price of purchasing the books.

Ingredients for Aaron's Marinated Salmon:
Cedar planks
1/3 cup Macadamia Nut Oil
1 1/2 tablespoons Rice Vinegar
1 1/2 tablespoons Mirin
1 teaspoon Sesame Oil
1/3 cup Soy Sauce, Light Soy Sauce, or Gluten-Free Soy Sauce
1/4 cup Green Onion
1 tablespoon Ginger (preferably grated fresh Ginger Root)
1 teaspoon Minced Garlic
2 pounds Salmon Fillets

Cooking instructions:
- Whisk wet ingredients, green onion, ginger, and garlic together in pan.
- Marinate fillets in a resealable bag for at least one hour, preferably three to six hours.
- Soak cedar planks in water for at least one hour.
- Turn on grill at medium.
- Place planks on grill for three minutes and then flip.
- Place salmon fillets on cedar planks skin down and close lid.
- Cook around eighteen minutes.

Tips:
No marinade can save salmon that is not fresh, so make sure you purchase fresh fish. I have been using macadamia nut oil for two years because of its added health benefits and high burning temperature. The secret will be out soon on this oil, and the kicker is it tastes like butter!

You can find cedar planks at your local grocery store or you can shop for them online. They will smoke, but they should not catch on fire if you soak them in water. I reuse the boards by washing them off with just water and then freezing them after cooking.

You can locate mirin and sesame oil in the Japanese section of your local grocery. Be careful with sesame oil. It is so tasty, but it has a very pronounced flavor; a little goes a long way.

Instead of grating my garlic and ginger by hand, I buy freshly ground tubes of the spices in the grocer's vegetable section. The green onion has to be finely minced to make sure the flavors are released, and be sure to thoroughly whisk all the ingredients in the marinade.

Finally, I use a vacuum marinating sealer, which opens the pores of the meat. This makes the process more thorough and take less time. You can search online for "vacuum sealer" or "vacuum marinade" and find quality products to help you with your marinating. For your information, though, a resealable zip top bag will also do the trick.

TRAINING

Instead of creating a specific training plan, this chapter takes a macro view on training. This lets you, the reader, decide if you can envision yourself tackling the intensity needed to have your body ready to compete with the best triathletes in the world. Even though I used to be a coach under the purplepatch umbrella, I would not presume to write a book on training that could fit everyone's needs. As with any training, there are many options that may be better suited for a specific individual's skill set, dedication, or goals.

One of the main reasons I wrote this manual was to extend my reach to those who could benefit from my advice in their pursuit of their triathlon goals. Getting coffee with everyone who wants to analyze training methods would be impossible, and it is tough for me to draw the line because I do enjoy helping people. If one sentence in this book cuts five minutes off someone's time, then I feel like it was worth writing.

Far too often, I find pro and amateur triathletes who believe their training is selfish. They see the amount of time they train as alienating their family and friends, and they feel like they lose touch with "real" life. However, it is not selfish to workout if it is your full-time job. Is it selfish to work on that business presentation to impress your boss? No. Performing well should be your goal, whatever your profession. Remember, this is your living, and triathletes put in their hours on the job the same way that others pound through a workweek. The key to any life is balance, and this is where the disconnect lies in the minds of some triathletes. The banker who is obsessed with work, leaving the house at seven o'clock in the morning and not returning until eleven that night, is the same as the triathlete who eats, sleeps, and breaths the sport; they are both setting themselves up for disaster.

I'd like to offer you a different perspective toward training and how it can fit into your life. Heck, I only workout (train) twenty-five hours a week, and some individuals work sixty hour work weeks! The time is available for you to have a balanced existence, so start becoming better at time management and prioritizing what is important in your life. Training can be an obsession, just like work, so it is up to you to recognize if you have a problem and to do something about it.

I usually workout twenty-five to thirty hours per week; some pro triathletes do more and some do less. When I was an age-grouper and rookie professional working sixty-hour weeks, I squeezed in fifteen hours of training, so going pro full time has freed up additional hours for me. I do still consider the amount of time I spend training on the low side for a professional triathlete, because I do most of my cycling indoors. I also practice quality over quantity because I know my body does not perform well with extensive training. There are some professional triathletes who respond well to running marathons on a consistent basis or riding outside for five or more hours multiple times a week. I never run more than fifteen miles in a run session, and I average one long three to five hour outdoor ride per week. I know I am in the minority as a pro for the number of training hours I put in. However, this is what I believe fits my schedule and body best.

In addition to the grueling length of the event and the need to be in constant motion, triathlon is a tough sport because you have to master three disciplines. Individually, swimming, running, and cycling are popular sports, and it takes a lot of practice to race competitively in any of them. If you are dedicated enough to become respectable at one of these disciplines, as a triathlete you now have to learn two additional, completely different sports that use other muscle groups. It is comparable to starting out using hand eye coordination to play basketball for an hour, then using your feet to play soccer for five hours, then ending up tackling, blocking, running, and throwing on the football field for three hours. Even the best athletes in the world would have a tough time being elite in all of these sports. Yet, this is what triathletes face when they embark on conquering their sport.

Most professional triathletes are above average in at least one of the three disciplines before jumping into the sport. I would say the majority of them have either a swimming or running background, and the bike is learned over time. Because of this inclination, it takes awhile for the physical aspects of these three sports to be in tune with each other, which also explains the number of years it takes for most triathletes to reach their peaks and perform at consistent levels. Also, people are drawn to triathlon because they want to tackle the difficulty of being good at three sports, and they attack the challenge with ferocity.

When athletes want to excel at triathlon, they take the logical steps to incorporate quality training regimens into their lives. So, failing as a triathlete is often due to things *other* than training. You need to examine everything surrounding the sport, besides training, to help you reach your triathlon goals. Training is controllable, and improvement is always apparent. Since you probably already have a training routine in place, I will look at each of the disciplines separately and present some conclusions I have drawn through my years as an amateur and pro.

Swim

Let's first take a bird's-eye view of the swim. From what I have observed, if you did not grow up swimming, it will be an uphill battle to be a competent swimmer. There is something that clicks when you learn certain sports at a young age; I put skiing, golf, and swimming in this category. The correct technique never leaves the child, and it is a lot easier to improve as you get older than it is to learn it for the first time at an older age. Skiing is a sport I started later in life, and no matter how hard I try, I am not as fluid as my friends who have skied since they were children. I ski probably six days a year, and I have no shot at achieving their levels. Now, if I were to move to a ski town and practice skiing for seventy days a season, I could make dramatic improvements. If people who have been skiing since childhood did this same training, they would still be better than me because they have the proper foundation and muscle memory ingrained in them.

I grew up swimming, and this has allowed me to excel in that segment of the triathlon. This is not to say I do not work at the discipline; I still spend countless hours in the pool. However, if you did not grow up swimming competitively and are looking to improve, you need to dedicate yourself to getting better. It will not just happen with increased repetition. Many pro triathletes who do not have a swimming pedigree take an entire off-season to work with a swim-stroke doctor. They practice regimented swimming, in both open water and lane swimming, to try to shave those precious minutes off of their overall times. The days of being a professional triathlete who is a slow swimmer are over. The top athletes are so strong in all three segments, your chance of finishing high in the top tier races will be slim if you are in the last pack of swimmers.

Although the swim is where you spend the least amount of time in the triathlon, it is important because the training helps you in the other two segments. The aerobic exercise in low impact water helps your fitness, while limiting the physical pounding your body endures from the bike and run. It is also mentally advantageous to not always be chasing your competition on the bike and run. The triathlon adage is, "The race is won on the run." To some extent this is true, but being in a good position out of the water can put you in a better place mentally and physically on the run.

In order to improve your swim, you need to be pushed. There was a period of ten years where I diligently swam the yardage needed to be good, but I was never pushed by better swimmers. My usual workouts would include one to two hours of swimming in a small lap pool, going back and forth like a hamster on a wheel in a cage. I maintained my fitness, but my muscles became accustomed to the pace, so I made no improvement. After I went pro and then freed up more time by quitting my day job, my coach at the time encouraged me to swim two times a week in a group. I also befriended former USA Olympic swimmer Dan Veatch, who allowed me to try to stay on his heels during workouts.

I went from swimming at a comfortable pace to being pushed by elite age-groupers in a controlled environment. Instead of using the swim as my mental relaxation time, I was now pushing myself to the verge of puking during group workouts (this is the satisfying type of puke feeling that comes with a quality workout). You need other people to push you, or you will never get better. Your muscle memory changes over time to incorporate this faster pace, instead of being lulled into stagnation by never-changing solo swim workouts. The results were that I shaved precious minutes off of my swim time, my confidence grew because I knew I could compete with the other elite triathlon swimmers, and I was able to transfer some of the energy I previously used to stay in the front pack on the swim to other areas of the race. I was expending less energy to achieve better results because of my more efficient swim strokes, which were a byproduct of being pushed in training.

Bike

Obviously, a quality swim is one of the keys to your race, but the top swimmers are not necessarily the ones finishing on the podium. The bike is the longest portion of the race, and there is no hiding a poor cycling performance. You can be one of the top swimmers and runners on the circuit, but if you have not learned how to cycle at a respectable level, you will never be able to make up the time in the other two disciplines.

The subtle nuances of proper cycling, combined with generating the power to propel your body and bike through the course, make it the most strenuous of the three events. What I mean by this is the amount of time you spend thinking, worrying, training, and fiddling with the bike before the event, plus the amount of time on the bike during the race, make it a huge time drain and an inefficient part of your life. This is not to say that struggling toward the finish line on the run is not strenuous, but it is a concentrated occurrence. Everything surrounding the bike is a constant worry throughout the season, which makes it, in my eyes, the most challenging to piece together. During the swim and run, your focus is on your own well-being. On the bike, you have to worry about the condition of your bike and outside forces on the road that have the potential to derail your race.

Although I am constantly looking for new ways to improve the aerodynamics of my bike through my riding technique and advancements in technology, my training has stayed consistent since I went pro. I do the majority of my bike training indoors in the San Francisco area. I teach and take multiple classes during the week that enable me to maintain my fitness and improve my power. Although this is the bulk of my training, I still get outside and practice in the environment in which I will race. There is no replacing road training to learn to deal with wind, pavement, the elements, hills, descents, and other riders. I train outside usually one day per week with a group of experienced riders to help push me on the route.

My cycling purist friends would say I am nuts because the reason they ride is to experience the great outdoors with their friends. I agree with this to an extent, and I cherish my outdoor rides on a beautiful Northern California day. However, my business is about efficiency, and my brand is about balance. Riding outside takes time, which is a precious commodity. If I could walk out my door, bike for a couple of hours, and then get on with my day, I would ride outside more often. However, most people do not have the luxury of accessible, challenging roads. Cutting out six hours of my day for travel to the ride, training, and travel home is not feasible on a daily basis.

I equate this quandary of whether to bike indoors or outdoors to golf. It is a joy to play eighteen holes on the weekend and make an event out of it. You play with your friends, work hard at your game together, and have a few drinks when it is done. However, it is not possible for most people to do this every day because the balance of their lives would be out of whack. It is more prudent to frequent the driving range or putting green to work on your game than it is to play a round. Consequently, you do want to justify your practice by going out on the course when possible, just like you want to be outside riding in the open air.

The advantage of training inside is you are pushed by your instructor to improve, and you feed off the energy of the like-minded individuals sweating away with you. If done correctly, the concentrated, efficient biking you do indoors is a more targeted workout than riding outdoors. You spend half the time indoors and reap the full benefits of a longer ride on the road. There is also something to be said for lessening the amount of time on the road to avoid potential crashes. I know you should not live your life in fear, but you can reduce the chance of injury if you concentrate the majority of your workouts indoors on a stationary bike. This does not totally prevent potential falls, as evidence by my two crashes in 2012, but the odds are lowered. It does frighten me to see the attitude of some drivers on the open road, the carelessness of some riders, and the narrow highways we traverse. There are a handful of close calls every ride, and one moment of lapse in concentration could be disastrous.

As with swimming, if you don't work out with individuals who are better than you, you won't be pushed, and you won't improve. This is especially true when you ride outdoors. If you are looking to improve your cycling, befriend individuals in your area who are comparable or better cyclers, and hit the road with them. You have to know what it is like to ride with people who are faster than you and who push you to keep up with them. This muscle memory will serve you well on race day. Riding with others in a community will allow you to pick up tips you might not have learned on your own.

I do my weekend rides with a posse of elite age group men, and it is a challenge to try to keep up with them. However, I have learned from these individuals, and their help made me into the cyclist I am today. They showed me that I could push power that I didn't think was possible. During my indoor sessions, I practice the techniques I learn with them, and I can see the steady improvement in the watts I generate, which validates these outdoor sessions. I seek out every opportunity to ride with fellow professional triathletes, and I try to pick up on their tendencies and how they are successful. I had an enjoyable ride with Chris Lieto who gave me some pointers on what made him revered in the cycling community and one of the best male cyclists in triathlon.

If you want to take large chunks off of your overall time, you should naturally concentrate on the event that is the longest. A triathlete recently approached me about trying to complete an Ironman in under ten hours, and I told him about power-based cycling sessions and how this could be his ingredient to achieving his goals. Power-based cycling workouts involve measuring and changing the watts you produced for an extended period of time. It is efficient, effective, and controlled. My husband and most of my pals are not in triathlon so I do not want to be on my bike seven hours every weekend day!

For example, you will do more work in a ninety-minute class than you ever would in ninety minutes outside. This length of class is like roughly riding for over three hours outside. Classes are usually one and a half to two hours each and we are on an eight-week rotation. For example, in winter months, it is all about zone two and three aerobic work. In the spring, we get into zone three and four threshold work. No matter what month, it is hard, efficient, effective stuff that targets all types of cyclists. For example, in my class, I love having members that are anywhere from a pro cyclist to a CEO of a company to a mom trying to get a great workout.

Run

There are some fast runners in the world of triathlon, and they are only getting faster. Mirinda Carfrae set the bar high in 2011 by running a 2:52:09 marathon at Ironman Hawaii. This was a record time for women at Kona, and only five professional males beat it that year. If you are not running under 3:10 marathons as a male or female, you will be hard pressed to podium in a full Ironman. This unbelievable running speed trend has consistently improved through all of the triathlon distances, so it is imperative you learn how to increase your speed in the marathon.

I do a lot of my running workouts on the treadmill. Once again, time is a valuable commodity, and I have access to a quality treadmill at my workout facility. I can roll out of bed and begin a workout in a matter of minutes. My running workouts are concentrated and efficient and allow me to avoid outside distractions such as stoplights, other runners, and obstacles. I am able to teach my muscles to move faster as I increase the speed of the treadmill, which is invaluable for improving my running. I am a big believer in showing your muscles that they can move faster, so that when the time comes to race, it becomes second nature to move at a faster pace. The result of doing a lot of my workouts indoors is I can complete swim, run, and bike training sessions within a few hours, since I can do everything within a two mile radius of my home.

Although running indoors is a big portion of my run training, just like cycling, I need training sessions outdoors that simulate my racing environment. The treadmill helps in speed muscle memory and fitness, but your body does need to train on pavement to become accustomed to a non-moving surface. The treadmill is more forgiving and has a different feel than the surfaces you will be running on in a race, and your body will react differently, so it is important to get used to this feeling. Most of my outdoor running is done after an indoor or outdoor cycling session to simulate running off the bike, as you would in a triathlon race. I usually do these types of workouts three times a week for thirty minutes to an hour. I also mix it up by sometimes doing an outdoor run session after my swim workouts. The key is to get your heart rate up with a long cycling or swim workout, and then quickly move into the outdoor running session. The more you can simulate during training how your body will feel during a race, the better you will respond during a triathlon.

I have also started incorporating sprint races in my run training, which I never did when I was an age-grouper. The result is that my body learns how to race faster, instead of always trudging along at an Ironman pace. Sprinting works different muscles than running. I would estimate that I have been sorer after sprinting a 10K or half marathon than racing a marathon because I am pushing my muscles out of their comfort zone. This work has enabled me to feel more comfortable on my longer Ironman distance runs, and I have developed more sustained speed than before I started more sprint training. There are hundreds of these types of sprint races throughout the year, so search for some in your area and sprinkle them into your schedule.

Running is a skill a lot of people have developed, but running successfully off of a long swim and bike ride is something that takes practice and time. Train to get the fitness that is required to complete the run, but remember it is only one third of the journey. How you perform on your swim and bike will inevitably affect your run, so pay attention to the details of those segments to make sure you are giving yourself the best possible chance to have a solid third leg of the race. This could include conserving your legs by not kicking as much on the swim, having the proper bike fit so your running muscles are not cooked by improper positioning, or strategically monitoring your watts in the bike race so you are not riding too hard. These "little things" can mean the difference between a strong finish to your race or struggling on the side of the road.

Weight and Core Training

No chapter about training can be comprehensive without discussing weight and core training. It is no secret you need to have a strong core as an athlete, especially in triathlon, where you are trying to master three distinctly different disciplines. I stopped weight lifting after college under the misconception that it made me bulky. In retrospect, it wasn't the lifting that increased my mass, but it was the type of lifting we were doing to increase our power in field hockey.

Core strength training was not part of my regimen as an age-grouper for six years because I did not know the proper way to go about it, and I did not realize how important it was to the sport. I concentrated on the swim, bike, and run but did not even think about weight training, which inevitably hurt my overall performance. You need a strong core to power through the swim, hold your position through long bike rides, and keep yourself upright on the run. A weak core puts strain on other muscles to accomplish the same tasks, which results in poor form, an unbalanced body, and an increased likelihood of injury.

When I went pro, I started to study other pro triathletes and how they approached weight training. The revelation for me was when TRX came onto the scene, and I studied the benefits of their core training, suspension trainer, and bodyweight resistance system. My realization was you could develop lean muscle mass using your own weight resistance, and the fear of bulking up was eliminated. I started using the TRX suspension trainer two to three times a week, and the improvements showed during my training and racing. This took about twenty minutes per session, so the time was minimal.

As the level at which I competed increased and running times kept dropping throughout triathlon, I knew I had to step up my core work to complement my bike to run transition. I began working with personal trainer and fitness expert Kate Ligler three years ago, specifically targeting my core to help me on the last few miles on the run and with power on the bike.

This training opened my eyes as to how off my body was in terms of how much stronger my dominant side was than the other. My back needed rebalancing because I was reliant on one side. We also targeted my core, which was crushed for a few weeks and then was able to "snap to" as it got used to actually being worked out and strengthened. For strength training in my legs, we targeted extension, which is the power to pull and extend the hamstrings. I was told my legs were in excellent strength to push, which is beneficial on the bike, so building up the extension strength will help give the run that extra kick. The weight training creates slimmer muscle fibers that are equally as strong as before.

The bottom line is I had to reset and reboot these muscle fibers to become more balanced. Working these dormant muscles created micro muscle tears resulting in initial fatigue and soreness, but the body is resilient and it comes back better than before. As the body continues to repair itself, it reprograms and become more balanced and, the net result, stronger. As I continue to work on these muscles, they begin to repair more easily, and hopefully I will have greater access to the muscle potential.

Coaches

Athletes derail their training when they do not follow their coaches' programs. If you put your faith in a coach and pay good money to receive weekly training plans, trust that the workouts will help you reach your goals. Give the program a year, and then evaluate your progress and make the decision if the coach you hired is the right one for you. Having been a coach, the problems I see usually lie in athletes thinking they are not doing enough volume, so they add workouts to the existing plan. This is equivalent to buying stocks in an account after hiring a money manager. Let the individual you hired do his or her job, and don't micro manage. See how the process unfolds before making any drastic changes.

Remember, your coach has other athletes and can't spend days talking about your every workout in detail. You should expect a plan every week, and I recommend touching base once a month and before a race to discuss strategy. It is natural to think you know what is best for your body, and sometimes your intuition may be right—just like you could pick a good stock every once in awhile. However, the overall plan is something that takes time, and you can eventually fall off track by adding an extra workout here or there. Just like a good money manager, a good coach has a plan. Neither can execute a plan properly if the client meddles with the product.

WEB—Why Even Bother?

You are not going to feel in top shape for every training session, and this is normal. However, it is still necessary to complete workouts when you don't feel up to it. These "Why Even Bother?" (WEB) workouts are the ones that build character and help you prove to yourself that you have the stuff to complete a race when inevitable adversity is present.

The best thing about WEBTASTIC workouts is that you need them to become a tougher athlete mentally, physically, and emotionally. I can't tell you how many WEB workouts I have endured...countless.

The reality is, sometimes you just don't have it! Your body cannot produce what the mind so vibrantly wants to, so you have to make adjustments...and this is OK! Sometimes the legs don't match the heart and vice versa. Thus, the best way to approach this is to dial down the power and get through the time of the session.

I find WEB workouts are one to two day stretches, and this is exactly when you have to listen to your body; this is a must! If we don't listen to our bodies, how will we ever grow? There is a time to push through the discomfort, and there is a time where you KNOW you cannot do it in that moment.

This happens on treadmill workouts, too, from time to time. An example is I get on the treadmill to do six six-minute miles and when I start the first one I know right away it isn't going to happen. I adjust and run zone one and two for the allotted time. I then do the correct workout on a day (usually the next) where I can, and that makes it all that much more productive and worthwhile.

The same thing can happen in the pool when we just don't have the fifth gear; it's all relative and it happens. It is 110 percent part of the sport and part of the training. Frankly, it's acceptable to have WEB days more frequently than not. You should not get discouraged because it's all part of the journey, the plan, and the process.

Discomfort

In training, you should get comfortable feeling uncomfortable. If you do not push yourself in your workouts to the point where you are questioning if you can continue, you will not improve. This includes regular and WEB workouts. If you are racing competitively in triathlon, you will be uncomfortable at many points during the event. You need to experience this feeling during your training, or you run the risk of failure.

As the saying goes, in triathlon, you truly need to "practice like you play." I often see individuals go through the motions in their training sessions. In their minds they have put in the time, shown up to the sessions, and completed the tasks. However, they have not pushed to improve. For years, I would swim aimlessly in the pool; I put in the time, but I never pushed myself to get better. I maintained my fitness and did more volume than a lot of triathletes, but I did not get the most out of the workouts to make gains on my time. Everyone gets comfortable in a routine. Break this comfort zone from time to time to work different muscles, try other activities, and take on new mental challenges. This will prepare you for race day.

When I was teaching I often had to encourage my clients to break their comfort zone to reach their next level. I'm sure some of you are thinking 'no way' can I do that (and I get that)…but trust me many of you will find the power and strength to do this. What I am suggesting is sometimes you need to embrace the 'comfortable feeling uncomfortable' to grow and become stronger athletes. I am not pushing this as a daily workout endeavor…overdoing it to the point of hurting yourself is not the object here…but pushing, now and then, and stepping back and saying 'hey, I survived that increase' will be good for your body and your mind. It will help you when you are in a crunch period during a race …you will remember you embraced the uncomfortable. It's those precious, subtle, mind-over-matter moments that create this huge platform for us to grow on and become even better and stronger riders and athletes—both mentally and physically.

I'm here to tell you…THAT YOU CAN!!!! Just let yourself try it and you'll be surprised that your body and mind can prevail…this I can promise you—even if you fail every now and then.

Recovery

A conversation about training can never be complete without talking about recovery. I couple the two concepts together because you cannot have successful training sessions without proper recovery. The subject is dealt with a few times in this manual because it is *that* important for a successful triathlon career. There are concepts the majority of triathletes understand such as sleep, light training days, and recovery protein shakes. However, I do feel you need to process, psychologically why a lot of triathletes fail at recovery, and I am including myself in this statement.

I view recovery like preventative medicine: practicing quality recovery will help you down the road, even if the benefits are not immediately evident. It is difficult for triathletes to fully focus on recovery because a common belief is if you are not training, you must be digressing. This is far from the truth, since recovery enables you to work harder in your training. However, the mind can get in the way of common sense. It is "cool" to talk with your friends and post online how you crushed yourself in a training session; it is not "cool" to let everyone know how you rested up and let your body heal. Your mind can latch on to your discussions about training with your competitors, but if recovery isn't brought up, then a very important part of the process is lost.

It was tough for me as an age-grouper, as well as pro triathlete, to know I needed more time to recover; especially as I get older. My brand is balance, but there are times when life gets in the way. The first thing to go in the chaos is recovery. What I have learned is to listen to my body; there is no set formula. Your coach should adequately sprinkle in recovery days and light training sessions, but it is up to you to not add workouts, to get the proper sleep, and to take the proper nutrients to allow your body to recover. One of the mantras that consistently goes through my mind is, "It takes confidence to recover." I build my training around this mantra and take the necessary steps to make it happen. I do not listen to what my competition is doing; instead, I concentrate on what I need to do to toe the starting line in the best position to succeed. This means having the discipline to let my body heal.

Favorite Workouts

The next section highlights a few of my favorite swim, bike, and run workouts; five in each modality. The goal is to show typical pro triathlete workouts in an average session. Some of the training language might be foreign to you, so I have included a brief glossary before each section. I love receiving emails from triathletes asking for guidance with their workouts, so here are some personal keepers!

Swimming
These workouts are all based on a 25-yard pool.
Meredith (MBK) swims: Favorite Swim Staple

We are starting out with two of my staple swim workouts before jumping into my five favorite. These types of swims are ones that I have done since my high school days and what we call 'MBK' swims. These can be anywhere from 5k-10k of straight swimming, back and forth back and forth, like a hamster on a spinning wheel. I absolutely love and embrace them even though they may seem to some as monotonous. I do a lot of these 'MBK' swims (4k-10k usually) when in between races one or two weeks apart and two to three times per week on a regular training basis. The other swims in the week are interval based. These help to maintain the resilience we need as triathletes and they are my chi time; mellow and relaxing which is comparable to yoga and stretching. I always look forward to these sessions!

SWIM: 2 days out from a race:
Swim: 1000 warm up easy swimming; every 4th lap non-free, loosen, smooth then:

8 x 25 build every 2 x 25's to the last 2 fast/take out speed on 5 seconds rest

Main prep: 4 x 600

600 pull (buoy/paddles/band) smooth at 70% effort

15 seconds rest

6 x 100 at 80% effort; goal is to 'feel good' on these

5 seconds rest between each

2 x 300 paddles and buoy only smooth at 70% effort

15 seconds rest between each

6 x 100 (odd - controlled take out speed at 90%; even - easy)

10 seconds rest between each

400 easy cool

TOTAL: 4000 yards

Favorite Swim Workouts:
Workout #1:

Warm up: 1000 smooth mix of strokes as you wish

Pre-Main Set #1:

200-175-150-125-100-75-50-25; all build in effort pulling with buoy/band/paddles

Pre-Main Set #2: *Swim*

4 rounds:

3 x 25's fast (5 seconds rest between each)

50 easy

Main Set: *Swim*

200's as:

1-1-1

1-1-2

1-1-3

1-1-4

1-1-5

(25 x 200's total)

- Note: You can make this set even 100's or 150's as the distance. The goal is for the first '1' to be *very easy* where you get nearly 20-30 seconds rest. The second '1' is to be *faster* yet still very smooth, likely getting around 5-7 seconds rest. The last 'x' number is to be *touch and go*; 1-2 seconds rest; threshold/race pace type speed.

100 easy cool
Total: 7500 yards

Workout #2:
Warm up: 1000 easy smooth free
Pre-Main Set #1: *Pull*
800 pull (paddles, buoy, band) build by 200 to strong.
20 seconds rest then:
Pre-Main Set #2: *Swim*
4 rounds:
2 x 25 fast (5 seconds rest between each)
50 easy
Main Set: *Swim*
2 rounds of:
300-300-300
200-200-200
100-100-100

- First 300/200/100 within each pocket should be *easy* with 15 seconds rest; 2nd 300/200/100 within each pocket should be *smooth* with 5-7 seconds rest; 3rd 300/200/100 within each pocket should be *fast* with 1-2 seconds rest

Continuous for two rounds
Cool down as you wish; 200 yards
Total: 6000 yards

Workout #3:
Warm up: 1000 swim; mix of strokes as you wish
Pre-Set: Fins on all

- Fins help promote leg recovery; I learned this from Gerry Rodrigues at Tower26: www.tower26.com

400 kick-swim by 25
400 swim smooth build by 100
200 kick-swim by 25
200 swim build by 50
Main: Twice through
50 *fast*, 100 at threshold (150 total at once) on 15 seconds rest
150 smooth 30 seconds rest
50 *fast*, 150 (200 total) at threshold on 10 seconds rest

150 *smooth* on 30 seconds rest

50 *fast*, 200 (250 total) at threshold on 5 seconds rest

150 *smooth* on 30 seconds rest

50 *fast*, 250 (300 total) at threshold on 1-2 seconds +Go...

150 *smooth* on 30 seconds rest

100 *easy* 30 extra seconds rest and then on to round 2

This is take out speed to threshold

5 x 200 pull with buoy/paddles/band to cool

100 *easy*

TOTAL: 6500 yards

Workout # 4: (Tower26 special!)

Warm up: 1000 swim; mix of strokes as you wish

Pre: 2 rounds: 400, 300, 200, 100 build effort

Round 1: Paddles and ankle strap

Round 2: Paddles only

Main: *Swim*

4 rounds of:

4 x 100 best effort on 45 seconds rest

4 x 100 buoy and snorkel at 60% on 15 sec rest

Looking for best sustainable pace/effort over each set of 4 x 100 fast and tough

300 cool

TOTAL: 6500 yards

Workout #5 (Tower26 special!)

Warm up: 1000 swim; mix of strokes as you wish

Pre-Main:

8 x 100 buoy/band/paddles at 70%

8 x 100 swim progress effort by 2's to 85% with 10 sec rest

Then 8 x 50 paddles only:

Odd: *Build*

Even: *Fast*

5-10 seconds rest between each

Main Set: *Swim*

Three rounds of:

10 x 50 yards with 30 seconds rest between each; absolute best effort with strong consistency

400 swim or pull; at recovery pace

Repeat for three cycles adding five seconds additional rest each cycle

300 extra cool down

TOTAL: 6000 yards

Biking

Glossary

Z = ZONE

L = LOW

M = MID

H = HIGH

PE = PERCEIVED EFFORT

RPM = REVOLUTIONS PER MINUTE

- ZONE 1: Easy and recovery; you could ride at this level all day (5/10 PE)
- ZONE 2: Endurance (HZ2/LZ3 = Ironman pace) (6/10 PE)
- ZONE 3: Strong and Controlled (HZ3=70.3 pace) (7/10 PE)
- ZONE 4: Threshold (8+/10 PE)
- ZONE 5: Heart out of chest hard (9+/10 PE)
- Example: LZ2 = Low Zone 2; HZ3 = High Zone 3

- CADENCE:
- BASE CADENCE = usually around 85 RPM (I am more like 80 RPM as I have a slow cadence)
- 5 RPM = 1 MPH
- MPH = Miles per hour
    - Example: If your BASE cadence is 18 MPH on your trainer, BASE+1 would be 19 MPH, BASE+2 would be 20 MPH, and BASE-2 would be 16 MPH
    - Example: If your BASE cadence is 85 RPM, BASE+1 would be 90 RPM, BASE+2 would be 95 RPM, and BASE-2 would be 75 RPM

Favorite Indoor Cycling Sessions:

Bike Session #1:

Warm up 30 minute *easy* ramping:

10 minutes Z1 high cadence (90+RPM or BASE+1)

10 minutes building by 2 minutes from LZ2-MZ3 your choice cadence

2 minutes *easy* then

6 minutes building by 2 minutes from MZ3-LZ4 your choice cadence

2 minutes *easy*

Then *big effort* as:

30 x 1 minute *very strong*; HZ4

1 minute off easy Z1: *maintain* tension on the chain HZ1; RPM should be over 85

- Note: 60 minute total set of 1 minute strong and 1 minute easy

5 minutes *easy* spin to flush legs then:

1 x 10 minute at L-MZ4 at *fast RPM* (over 95 is ideal)

Then cool 10 minute easy Z1

Bike Session #2:

Warm up 10 minutes at Z1 easy spinning before:

5 minutes - 4 minutes - 3 minutes - 2 minutes - 1 minute

1 minute Z1 continuous easy spinning between each

- 5 minutes building from LZ2-HZ2; 4 minutes building from MZ2-LZ3; 3 minutes building from HZ2-MZ3; 2 minutes building from LZ3-LZ4; 1 minute building from LZ4-HZ4

Cadence builds from Base cadence to Base+3 within each interval

- Reminder: Base = about 85 cadence (RPM); so Base+1 = 90 RPM, Base+2 = 95 RPM; Base+3 = 100 RPM

Main Set: 4 x 9 minutes as:

#1 Climbing:

2 minutes HZ3 Base-2 (75 RPM)

2 minutes LZ4 Base-4 (65 RPM)

2 minutes MZ4 Base-6 (55 RPM); can go in and out of the saddle every

20 seconds
2 minutes HZ4 Base-6 for 30 seconds, Base-4 for 30 seconds, Base-2 for 30 seconds, Base for 30 seconds THEN:
1 minute LZ1 *fastest sustainable cadence you can hold* at this lower power (Base+5 or 110 cadence)

4 minutes *easy* Z1 spinning

#2 Steady State:
2 minutes HZ3 Base+2 (95 RPM)
2 minutes LZ4 Base+3 (100 RPM)
2 minutes MZ4 Base+3 (105 RPM)
2 minutes HZ4 Base+5 for 30 seconds, Base+5 for 30 seconds, Base+3 for 30 seconds, Base+2 for 30 seconds, then:
1 minute LZ1 *fastest sustainable cadence you can hold* at this lower power (Base+5 or 110 cadence)

4 minutes *easy* Z1 spinning

#3 Climbing:
1 minute HZ3 Base-2 (75 RPM)
1 minute LZ4 Base-3 (70 RPM)
3 minutes MZ4 Base-4 (65 RPM); can go in and out of the saddle every 20 seconds
3 minutes HZ4 Base-6 (55 RPM) for 30 seconds, Base-5 for 30 seconds, Base-4 for 30 seconds, Base-3 for 30 seconds, Base-2 for 30 seconds, Base-1 for 30 seconds then:
1 minute LZ1 *fastest sustainable cadence you can hold* at this lower power (Base+5 or 110 cadence)

4 minutes *easy* Z1 spinning

#4 Steady State:
1 minute HZ3 Base+2 (95 RPM)
1 minute LZ4 Base+3 (100 RPM)
2 minutes 30 seconds MZ4 Base+3 (105 RPM)
3 minutes 30 seconds (HZ4 Base+3 for 60 seconds, Base+4 for 60 seconds, Base+5 for 60 seconds, Base+6 for 30 seconds) then:

1 minute LZ1 *fastest sustainable cadence you can hold* at this lower power (Base+5 or 110 cadence or faster)

4 minutes *easy* Z1 spinning

Bike Session #3:
5 minutes *easy* spin in Z1
Pre-Main Set:
2 by 3 minutes
2 by 2 minutes
2 by 1 minute
With 1 minute in Z1 in between each
Odd: Z2 RPM ramp from BASE (85 RPM) to BASE+4 (105 RPM)
Even: Power builds from LZ2 to MZ4; your choice RPM
Smooth quick openers to get ready for the main set of:
60 minutes continuous pedaling:

10 minutes as:
2 minutes Z2 choice RPM
2 minutes Z3 drop cadence to Base-5 (60 RPM)
2 minutes Z3 seated climb as Base-7 (50 RPM)
2 minutes Z3 ramp to BASE cadence

2 minutes *easy* Z1

4 by 1 minute HZ4
1 minute *easy* at Z1 between *each*
Keep RPM on these at your most efficient pedal stroke comfortable for you at this power

8 minutes as:
4 minutes HZ2 rollers
- Note: A roller is 1 minute at 20 seconds at BASE, 20 seconds at BASE-2; 20 seconds at BASE-4; 20 seconds at BASE-6 climbing *out* of the saddle, 20 seconds build to BASE, 20 seconds BASE+3 thus, do 2 rollers within these 4 minutes.
2 minutes MZ3 *steady state*; your choice RPM
2 minutes HZ3 *fast* RPM (Base+3+++)

2 minutes Z1 *easy*

4 by 90 seconds at HZ4
Keep RPM on these at *your* most efficient pedal stroke comfortable for you at this power.
1 minute Z1 between each

6 minutes as:
2 minutes LZ3 BASE-5 (60 RPM)
2 minutes MZ3 BASE-7 (50 RPM)
2 minutes HZ3 ramp back to BASE cadence (80-85RPM)

4 by 2 minutes at HZ4
Keep RPM on these at *your* most efficient pedal stroke comfortable for you at this power.
1 minute Z1 between each

4 minutes *build* in power and cadence from LZ2-HZ3 and from BASE to BASE+6

Cool down 5-10 minutes

Bike Session #4:
Warm up: 10 minute easy spin in Z1

Pre-Main:
2 x 4 minute ramp Z2 from BASE to BASE +5
2 x 3 minute ramp Z2 to Z3/4
2 x 2 minute ramp Z2 to Z3/4 and BASE to BASE + 5
Continuous

Pre-Main #2:
2 x 6 minute prep – your choice cadence
1.5 minute each as: MZ2, HZ2/LZ3, MZ3, LZ4. = 6 minutes
2 minute spin in Z1 between each

Main: 5 rounds of:

1 minute HZ4/LZ5 to Z5 *fast* RPM
1 minute 30 seconds MZ3 form riding choice RPM 4 minute spin Z1 recovery

Final Set:
3 x 9 minute Z1 with every 3rd minute as 30 sec at Z5 *fast* RPM
2 minute spin between each in Z1

Bike Session #5: (purplepatch special!)
Warm up: 10 minute easy spin in Z1

Pre-Main:
1 x 4 minute ramp Z2 from BASE to BASE +3
2 x 3 minute ramp Z2 to Z3/4 from BASE to BASE+4
3 x 2 minute ramp Z2 to Z3/4 and BASE to BASE + 5.
Continuous

Pre-Main #2: (9 minutes total)
1 x 6 minute prep; your choice RPM
1 minute 30 seconds MZ2, HZ2/LZ3, MZ3, HZ4
3 minute spin *easy* following

Main:
Set one: 4 x (40 sec Z5 [max sustainable effort] fast rpm, 3 minute easy Z1)
Recovery: 5 minute Z1 spin.
Set two: 4 x (30 sec Z5 [max sustainable effort] fast rpm, 3 minute easy Z1)
Recovery: 5 minute Z1 spin.
Set three: 4 x (20 sec Z5 [max sustainable effort] fast rpm, 3 minute easy Z1)

5 minutes *cool down* in Z1

Running
Treadmill Workouts: Use these arbitrary zones as examples; you can adjust according to your skill level.

Z1: 8:00 minutes per mile
Z2: 7:55-7:20 minutes per mile
Z3: 7:15-6:35 minutes per mile
Z4: 6:30-6:00 minutes per mile
Z5: Sub 6:00 minutes per mile

Z= ZONE
L=LOW
M=MID
H=HIGH
PE = PERCEIVED EFFORT

Treadmill Workout #1
Warm up 1 mile at Z1 pace
6 minutes at LZ3 pace, 3 minutes at Z1 minute pace
5 minutes at MZ3 pace, 2 minutes and 30 seconds at Z1 minute pace
4 minutes at HZ3 pace, 2 minutes at Z1 minute pace
3 minutes at LZ4 pace, 1 minute and 30 seconds at Z1 minute pace
2 minutes at MZ4 pace, 1 minute at Z1 minute pace
1 final minute at HZ4 pace

- Cool down 1 mile at whatever pace you desire. You just need to make sure you are *running* through this entire session even if that means going more than 8 minute miles during these recovery sessions.

Treadmill Workout #2
Warm up 2 miles at Z1 pace
12 x 2 minutes (first 6 intervals at MZ4 pace, last 6 intervals at HZ4 minute pace; 30 seconds straddle in between each
Jog 5 minutes at whatever pace you want to recover then:
6 x 1 minute at Z5 minute pace; 30 seconds straddle in between each
2 miles *easy* (running in Z1 pace)

Treadmill Workout #3
Warm up 1 mile at Z1
Build 15 minutes: 5 minute at LZ2, 5 minutes at MZ2, and 5 minutes at HZ2
2 minutes at cool down pace Z1

10 minutes MZ3
2 minutes at cool down pace Z1
4 x 3 minutes at Z4 pace; jog 2 minutes at Z1 in between each
10 minutes at HZ3
Cool down 1 mile at whatever pace is relaxing and comfortable
Stretch and done

- The two 10 minute intervals are to be about a 7-8/10 effort
- The 3 minute intervals should be 8-9/10 effort; these are those quick and efficient workouts that triathletes *must* do.

Treadmill Workout #4
Warm up 2 miles at Z1 pace
4 x 4 minutes set as:
4 minutes at HZ3 pace
4 minutes easy (Z1)
4 minutes at LZ4 pace
4 minutes easy (Z1)
4 minutes at MZ4 pace
4 minutes easy (Z1)
4 minutes at HZ4 pace
4 minutes easy (Z1)
1 more mile (after final 4 minutes easy) at whatever pace is relaxing and comfortable

Treadmill Workout # 5
Warm up 1 mile at Z1 minute pace then:
6 x 5 minutes; 3 minute jogs at Z1 minute pace in-between each 5 minute interval
1st 5: HZ2 pace
2nd 5: LZ3 pace
3rd 5: MZ3 pace
4th 5: HZ3 pace
5th 5: LZ4 pace
6th 5: MZ4 pace
Do two rounds of this if you need more volume
Warm down 1 mile at Z1 minute pace and stretch

Track Workout #1

Warm up: 2 miles easy Z1

Pre-Main Set: 1 x 6 minute build by 1 minute 30 seconds from Z2 to a strong Z3 effort

Main Set:
2 x 2000 meters
2 x 1600 meters
2 x 1200 meters
2 x 800 meters
All of these at 70.3 race pace
400 meters Z1 easy between each

Track Workout #2
Track Pyramid
Warm up: 2 miles easy Z1 then:

Main set:
400 meters
800 meters
1200 meters
1600 meters
2000 meters
2000 meters
1600 meters
1200 meters
800 meters
400 meters
200 meters easy between each
All at desired 70.3 race pace

RACE WEEK

Race week! The week that affirms your hard work has paid off. This is not the time to slack. My race week consists of a highly regimented routine stemming from years of practice, failure, and success. As with anything, if you do it enough, you get a sense of what puts you in the optimal position to do your best. There are inevitable stresses surrounding a race; the key is to minimize these with proper preparation. You want to go through race week knowing as much as possible about your itinerary. This will help you avoid some of the headaches that come with traveling, sponsor and media obligations, and lodging in a different environment.

This section is laid out chronologically, beginning with pre-race-week tasks, ending with post-race recovery and assessment. Race week ends with your race, so if your race is on a Sunday, race week begins the previous Sunday. Obviously, you have been following your coach's training plan, and depending on the training philosophy, you will continue working out through the week up until race day. As I have mentioned, my routine does not involve tapering. If I have a balanced training regimen, my race should be another blip on the road to optimal performance. I always want to be improving through the offseason and season, so a good training routine should take this into account. I will have workouts all the way up until the day of the race and then a flush out the day after the race. This may seem like a contradiction to a lot of athletes' workout programs, but it is what keeps me focused on my overall performance and not just one race on the radar. The training plan should prepare you to be in your best condition around race time, so it is not prudent to schedule a fifty-mile bike ride days before the race. But by keeping the body in motion, you will hit the ground running at the event.

Pre-Race Preparation
In reality, race week preparation began at the beginning of the season

with your training. If you have trained properly, you should arrive at race week ready to propel yourself through the event. Hopefully you are confident enough in your coach's plan and your fitness that it is not an area of stress. There are so many things to worry about this week, if you come in unfit and unconfident in your abilities, your stress levels will be off the charts, which will hamper your racing. Because of the time drain of my day job while an age-grouper, one of my prime worries was definitely whether or not I had the fitness to compete. As a pro, I trust I have put in the time, effort, and training to toe the line. However, adversity is always lurking around corners, and misfortunes such as injuries, sickness, or your period can always derail the best-laid plans.

Weather

I monitor the weather conditions surrounding the event about three weeks out because it is a natural occurrence out of your control. I train in extremely moderate temperatures in San Francisco, with very little exposure to intense heat, so it is imperative I properly prepare for the weather before I race. I train in a heated pool and at room temperature in my cycling studio and treadmill. My outdoor bike rides are conducted in the cool mornings, and occasionally the temperature gets to ninety degrees Fahrenheit in the afternoon. Needless to say, if the humidity and heat is soaring at a race, I need to prepare for this type of weather or I will falter. I can look at my splits from different races, and it is easy to see which ones had extremely high temperatures.

The reality is, I perform better in cooler weather because of my build and the conditions in which I train. I like to say "my junk in the trunk" helps me during cool morning race swims, rainy weather, and cloud cover days. Other racers who are smaller boned or built for running get very uncomfortable with race conditions like this, but I am in my element. You have to monitor the weather because your body type, training conditions, and inclination toward warm or cool weather racing dramatically affect you on race day. If you enter a race not knowing what that day's weather forecast is, one third of the time you will be all right if there are perfect conditions. However, one third of the time it will be very hot and one third of the time it will be cooler than normal. Do you really want to just roll the dice on race day? If you prepare for the race conditions, you have eliminated a stress factor that could destroy the race you have trained so long and hard to complete.

There is no hidden secret to cold or rainy weather. You have to stay warm. If you are not properly prepared for these conditions, you may experience any number of issues, like uncontrollable chattering, bad decision-making, cramping, and even hypothermia. You may not be able to hold on to the handlebars on the bike, and energy normally used for exercise will be used for warming your body. It is necessary to wear a hat covering your ears in the morning as you arrive at the race. Layers are a must so you can add and subtract as needed. Warm up for at least fifteen minutes to get the blood flowing and have another shirt to change into after the warm-up to keep your sweat from cooling you. Once you put on your wetsuit, be sure to wear your swim cap to keep the heat in. I also wear socks until I get into the water to keep my feet warm. Tread water to keep the blood flowing and flex muscles to make them work to generate heat.

I usually do not wear sleeves when I ride, even on cold mornings, because my body temperature naturally runs high. I fear overheating more than being cold on the bike, and for me, being too warm can make for an uncomfortable ride and a disastrous run. What requires warmth on the bike are your extremities. It is imperative on cold days to wear bike gloves, a fresh pair of socks, and an aero helmet with earflaps. The bike gloves are important because you cannot steer if your hands cannot grip the handlebars, which is dangerous. I would buy a cheap pair of wool gloves for cold days and get a more expensive set for rainy conditions. If your hands and feet are cold then the rest of your body will be cold, so dry socks are important, even if they eventually get wet. Starting out after a long, cold swim is where you are most susceptible to being miserable the entire bike ride.

On the run, depending on the length of the race, I change into a fresh pair of socks, which is always an uplifting treat. If it is raining, I have double wrapped my gear in transition because I have found the bags provided by the races are not completely waterproof. If you had to rack your bike and gear the night before the event and it is raining, double bagging is a necessity to ensure your bike and run gear are not completely soaked, which can be the difference between a good and bad race. Some individuals wear calf or arm sleeves, but I have never felt the need for them. At this point in the race, if my core temperature is not hot, nothing will get it up.

When I look at the weather three weeks in advance of a race, I concentrate on the heat and humidity. The weather outlook will determine if I need to do my heat training prior to the event, or I risk not being able to cope with the heat. If it will be cold, it is business as usual. I have a friend who lives and trains in Phoenix, Arizona, and it is cold to her when the weather dips below seventy-two degrees Fahrenheit. My friend literally has to put layers on at that temperature but feels at home in ninety-degree heat; that is what this individual is used to. This is how intense heat training is on the body. It took me years to figure out how to adapt to warmer weather, especially temperatures over ninety degrees Fahrenheit and high levels of humidity. I will share some of my tricks for adapting to higher heat than you are accustomed to.

I use sauna heat training to adjust my body to try to reach maximum performance in higher temperatures. There is a sauna near my treadmill facility, so I have convenient access to complete my conditioning. *Be sure to consult your doctor before attempting sauna heat training.* Below is my method for heat conditioning.

- Start sauna training seven days before heading to the race site.
- You should choose a training session where you have close access to a sauna. It does not matter if it is after a swim, bike, run, or weight-lifting session. The key is to make sure your heart rate is up.
- Fuel normally during your training session.
- Enter the sauna up to twenty minutes after the training session, but try to do it immediately.
- Do not rehydrate.
- You can have a small snack to refuel.

- The sauna session should be at least fifteen minutes and no longer than thirty minutes.
- The sauna temperature can be in the range of 158 and 185 degrees Fahrenheit.
- Wait ten to fifteen minutes after the sauna to begin rehydration.
- You should do a gradual rehydration the next four hours.
- Repeat this daily for seven days.

The key with sauna training is to simulate hot race conditions. The body is dehydrated from a training session, and you are now exposing it to high heat. Your body will adjust to the higher temperatures over time so it feels less stress overall. Further exposure over the course of a week will help your body deal with the core temperature rise and help reduce this increased stress rate. You shouldn't hydrate fully after the sauna treatment because this will lessen the alteration effect. Hydrate slowly over the next few hours, sipping small amounts of fluid regularly. Remember, you should stay hot as long as you feel comfortable and no more than thirty minutes. Be careful if you have injuries or wounds; do not use sauna heat training if they are extensive.

Two weeks before the race, you can also begin taking five hundred milligrams of magnesium for a week. If you keep your magnesium levels up, your potassium stays with it and the reverse is true. You can stop a week out so as to not upset your stomach on race day; high levels can cause diarrhea. You can get potassium through foods like bananas, avocados, and nuts. It is essential for regulating total body water and stabilizing muscle contractions, which are obviously important for endurance athletes. You lose both supplements through sweat. If your magnesium levels are not regulated, your potassium will suffer, which will hurt you on hot race days. This symbiotic relationship is real. Even if you consume potassium, it will go through your body faster if your magnesium levels are not kept up. *As with any supplement, consult your doctor before consuming it and practice before doing it for the first time at least two weeks before a race.*

The last step in my heat adaptation takes place on race day. The run is usually the hottest portion of the event since it takes place during the hottest part of the day, so this is where the majority of casualties lie. I freeze some water bottles the night before the race and put them in my run bag and strategically position one in my shirt and carry the other one. The bottles should still be cool by the time you get to them on the run in a full Ironman. Also, you should not start out the run by popping your champagne cork meaning do not go out too fast; pacing is a huge tactic on hot days. This allows you to ease into the heat.

My breakthrough moment in using these methods and successfully racing in the heat was at EagleMan in 2012. The race conditions called for a typical Eastern Shore of Maryland summer day, which is hot and very humid. I followed all of my heat instructions and was able to power through the run in ninety- five-degree temperatures with atypically high humidity. The run was definitely uncomfortable, but the heat training helped me overcome this. I took away from this event that I needed to hydrate almost one and a half times my normal amount during my training sessions leading up to the event and during the race. I was overly conscience of the fact my body was losing a lot of water, so I made it a point to sip liquids during the night before the race, drink up until the swim start, refill my water bottles on the ride, and stop at every aid station on the run. I was amazed at the amount of liquid I consumed, but it was necessary for me to do this to compete at a high level in the heat. If you do not adjust your liquid consumption when competing in heat intensive conditions, you run the risk of dehydration.

Checklists

By following the steps above, I try to be as prepared as I can be for unpredictable weather. I have created race-week checklists for the things I can control. How many times have you gone to an event only to forget an important item necessary for your race? This inevitably creates unneeded mental stress, which takes an unmeasured toll on the body. I institute a simple tool that people use in their everyday lives: the checklist. I systematically go through every item and check it off as I pack. This isn't rocket science, yet I always hear of someone forgetting something important at every race. If you take meticulous care making sure everything you need is actually packed, it will be one less thing occupying your mind when you should be concentrating on hydration, nutrition, and your race strategy.

I have two checklists I always complete when racing: one is the race trip checklist before I travel to the event, and the other is the race morning checklist I complete the day before the race. I have uploaded these lists onto the Life of a Triathlete website, www.lifeoftriathlete.com, in PDF and Excel formats for you to use and adjust for your racing needs.

Race Trip Checklist
Gear
Bike charger for components
Bike computer
Bike shoes
Calf sleeves
Camera and battery charger
CO2 cartridges
Headlamp (looking at bike race morning)
Helmets—aero and regular
Laptop and charger
Money
Music player and charger
Phone and charger
Vittoria Pit Stop Flat Fix Road Racing Bicycle Tire Inflator
Pre-race and recovery wraps (Arctic Ease)
Race numbers and timing chip
Racing wheels
Recovery Boots
Registration confirmation
Running shoes
Sunglasses
Sunscreen
Swim cap
Swim goggles
Tattoos—sponsors
Tire pump
Tires and spare tubular tires
Tools—bike
USAT Membership Card

Watches—GPS
Water bottles
Wetsuit—regular and speedsuit

Clothing
Extra racing clothes
Hat/visor
Hoodies
Jeans or sweat pants
Race number belt
Racing kit
Running shorts (x number of days)
Running top (x number of days)
Shoes
Socks
Swimsuit
Towels
Travel (airplane) clothes (two sets)
Wristband

Nutrition
Gels and Blocks
Food shopping list
Hydration drink
Mustard packets
Protein drink
Salt tabs
Sodium drink
Vitamins/supplements and case

Miscellaneous
Course maps
Curling iron
Driver's license
Driving directions and maps to venues
Eye mask—sleeping
Hairbrush
Hotel confirmation

Melatonin (sleeping aid)
Passport (if applicable)
Plastic baggies
Phone changed to international (if applicable)
Race instructions (race packet)
Rental car confirmation
Rings
Safety pins
Sharpie
Shaving cream
Wallet

I suggest using my list as a reference and tweaking it to fit your needs. The categories of gear, clothing, nutrition, and miscellaneous should be universal, but the contents will change based on gender and the individual needs of the athlete. If you follow the list protocol when heading to a race, you should have everything you need to compete, which alleviates the potential headache of running around trying to find items you forgot. Once again, my brand is balance, and in order to achieve this balance, I need to be organized. Even the slightest misstep can add stress to your race week; this hurts your mental preparation, which can ultimately hurt your race.

I take care of my race morning checklist the afternoon before the race. Depending on if you have to rack your bike the day before or morning of the race will determine when some of these tasks are accomplished. As with the race trip checklist, everyone's needs are different; this should be used just as a reference and be tweaked to fit your needs. Please note this is for a full Ironman.

Race Morning Checklist
Refrigerator
Two bottles full of hydration drink (one hand grip holder)
One bottle full of water

Freezer
One bottle full of hydration drink for bike special-needs bag
One small bottle of hydration drink for run transition gear bag

One small bottle of hydration drink for run special-needs bag

Gear/Items
Sponsor tattoos
Timing chip on ankle
Sunscreen (to apply after tattoos)
Charging bike computer
Charging components battery
Pump
Special-needs bags
Wedding ring to husband

Things to do
Drop off special-needs bags
Put frozen water bottle in run gear bag
Put computer on bike
Put component battery on bike
Cut Block packages and put them in bento box
Put BASE Electrolyte Salt/gum in bento box
Check and pump tires
Warm up jog
Bottles in bike frames
Bottle in Aerodrink Bracket
Apply sunscreen

The last thing you should be worrying about before a race is a small detail like whether you have enough water bottles or sunscreen. Take the time to properly set out the gear, check items off your list, and try to get some sleep. If you have ever seen great public speakers, the one characteristic they all share is preparedness. A prepared person exudes confidence, and this is the same way you should approach your triathlon before a race. If you make sure all the little things are taken care of, you will be more confident on race day. It always pains me to see athletes frantic a few days before a race because they did not take the time to find out where they were going, read the rules, pack the correct gear, or have their race paraphernalia meticulously laid out before the event.

Scheduling

As with weather preparation, you need to schedule the many race-week components weeks, or even months, in advance to make sure you are not running around like a chicken with its head cut off that week. The lists I mention above are the items needed so for your race to begin without a hitch. The scheduling for race week is what allows you to be more comfortable leading up to the race so that you are in a positive frame of mind. Have you ever traveled to a city you've never been to before and not known where you are going? It is frustrating. You get angry, you may lash out at your significant other who is driving, and, if you have to be somewhere, your anxiety is tripled. Have you ever reserved a hotel room only to find out it doesn't have Wi-Fi or the Internet costs $20 per day? This is a minor annoyance, but it causes angst nonetheless. There is a tension that cannot be seen or measured, and I am a big believer that all of this adds up to ultimately affecting how you perform. Why not try to keep these annoyances to a minimum?

Organizing

First, I want to discuss *why* it is important to be prepared for a race, not just physically, but organizationally. The biggest unknown of your racing ability is the effect of mental stress. I absolutely despise the word "stress" because it means life is getting the better of you and you are having a tough time coping with your situation. However, there is no denying that, even small detours in your planning, can stew in your mind, taking your focus off of the task of accomplishing your goal of having a solid race.

I have seen racers, including myself, come into race week in optimal physical condition but perform below their standards for what may seem like unknown reasons. You have to take a step back and take a view of your mental state to see if this was a culprit in fatiguing your body. Was your mind constantly churning through all of your chores you had not accomplished? Did you have trouble sleeping because you were worrying about when and where you needed to be? How many directions were you pulled due to family, friend, or sponsor obligations? Although these might seem trivial, your body is directly affected. This is the equivalent of taking a weekend ski trip with family and friends before an important presentation on Monday. You may think the trip turned out fine when you arrived home on Sunday night with the family intact and no broken bones. Yet the next day you feel sluggish during the presentation because over the weekend your mind was focused on the drive, the kids fighting, meeting up with your friends on the mountain, making sure everyone is having fun, hotel accommodations, getting the kids dressed in their gear, etc.

I came into the Vegas 70.3 Worlds in 2012 almost fully recovered from breaking my back. However, my mental fatigue was high, and I overextended myself before the event. The result was a poorly executed, dehydrated race. My body, although almost fit, was worn down from mental fatigue. I agreed to do multiple interviews, sponsor obligations, and family and friend lunches when I should have been hydrating, eating, and resting. I was driving around without knowing where I was going, sprinting to register and check my transition bags, squeezing in workouts that were on my plan in extremely hot temperatures, and returning emails at night when I should have been sleeping. All of these factors, combined with an extensive rehab period to get me to a race-ready position, led to my body breaking down on race day. I did not realize the extent that my poorly planned schedule played in my racing until a few days later when I had a chance to take a step back and figure out what went wrong. I guarantee if I had a do-over, I would have recognized my mental state, cancelled my obligations, hydrated properly, and rested in my room in my Recovery Boots.

Trip Planning

The scheduling tips I relate below may be second nature to some triathletes, but I am including them for the people who have asked me, "How do you do it?" After reading this section, take note of the tasks you actually accomplished before a particular race and the ones where you may have fallen short. See if it caused you unnecessary anxiety. The goal is to toe the line with a fresh body and mind, and simply taking the extra time to research your hotel or print out directions could help you in your race. Once again, you can't measure mental anxiety, thus, eliminate as much of it as possible to set yourself up for a better race experience.

Once I know I am entering a race, I look for sleeping accommodations as soon as possible. A lot of races fill up quickly, which means thousands of athletes and their families will be flooding the hotels in the area. Get booked early to avoid the pitfalls of having to locate a residence at the last minute. I make sure the place has Wi-Fi included in the cost of the hotel. I also check to see if it has a kitchen, freezer, and refrigerator. I like to eat some meals "in" if I can, plus I need these features for my pre-race breakfast. I also freeze water bottles before the race so they are cool when I end up using them on the course. I make sure the room has two queen beds to avoid another kicking body when I am trying to get my sleep before the event. Even small disturbances in the REM sleep cycle from someone else's movement can disrupt an otherwise peaceful night's rest. I have also grown accustomed to a white noise machine that hums to block out any extra night noises. You can find these online for a fairly cheap price. The goal is to make your accommodations as close to what you are used to as possible; comfort is a key component when preparing for a race.

The next step is to secure transportation. I need a vehicle wherever I race because I have sponsor obligations at different locations, and I need to transport the bike for riding and tune-ups, go grocery shopping, and make sure I stay off my feet by efficiently completing my tasks. I signed up for Avis Preferred, which is free and allows you to check in and out quickly. I also utilize the many rental car discount codes floating around the Internet to locate cheaper vehicles. I require a mid- to full-size SUV so I can transport my bike in the box or fully built. You shouldn't need to purchase the optional insurance based on your own car insurance or the one provided by the credit card you use. However, research this before renting, especially in foreign countries. Hopefully, your phone has a GPS application, but if not, purchase the GPS addition on your rental car to ensure you know where you are going.

I know this is the paperless age; nevertheless, I still create a physical packet for each race. This includes all directions to the events, including from the rental car location to the race site and hotel, hotel to race site, hotel to sponsor obligations, hotel to a local pool and biking and running paths, hotel to Whole Foods or a local grocery store, and hotel to my favorite restaurants for pre-race eating. I am partial to Outback Steakhouse because I know I can get chicken and a sweet potato to fuel me for the race, so I seek out the ones in the area and make sure I know how to get there. I also print the important pages of the athlete race guide provided by the event, which are usually found on their website. This includes rules, maps of the course and race site, and the schedule of events. As a backup, all of this information is also accessible on my mobile device, but I like to have the packet in my backpack at all times. Once again, these little details add to my efficiency during race week. Nothing is more frustrating than driving around a city you are not familiar with trying to locate the swim start or a healthy place to eat.

Once I have ground transportation, I then have to schedule my flight. I like to arrive a few days in advance, because race and sponsor obligations are usually two days before the event. I want time to get settled in my pre-race routine. I try to schedule my flight out a few hours after the awards (got to think positively!) unless I am tacking a few extra days on the back end to relax. As a reminder to age-groupers at Ironman events, you have to be present at awards to accept your Kona slot if you qualified. Too many times I have seen athletes leaving before accepting their Kona invitations, and their spots are rolled down to others who are present.

The flight planning is a delicate balance of timing, availability, mileage discounts, and luck. In reality, you can spend hours trying to save fifty dollars on a flight, but this is inefficient if your time is worth maybe one hundred dollars an hour. I usually check my miles, a few flight search engines, and a flight predictor website to see if I should wait on purchasing, and then I pull the trigger. I always attempt to reserve direct flights; this alleviates the chance of losing my bags when changing planes. Another check off my stress list! I like to fly United because Aaron and I have high enough status to get one free bag each, and we both travel with huge Saucony bags full of all my gear. I pack a carry-on with essential race gear, one day's attire (workout and regular clothing), and expensive items I can't afford to lose. With my status, I have priority boarding, which allows me to stow this important bag above me and not run the risk of having it put underneath out of my possession. However, this luxury is not available to me on every airline. I purposely choose an aisle or middle seat next to my husband by the bathroom because I will, and should have to, pee frequently. Once again, when you can eliminate the stress of the little things, such as worrying about multiple trips to the bathroom, your body will thank you on race day.

My race schedule was given to my sponsors before the beginning of the season and they usually reach out to me before an event they are attending to see if we can work out a meeting, interview, or appearance. These should be scheduled in advance so you can prepare for them and set appropriate time limits to make sure you are off your feet in a cool, controlled environment prior to your race. It does throw you off your routine if you get asked to do something last minute in a time slot that was designated for relaxation. I have learned to sometimes say "No" after my experience at the 70.3 World Championships in 2012. You may not think an hour interview or appearance would be draining, but it is mentally demanding. It is part of the job to schedule some meetings and events, but it behooves you to not overextend yourself, as a pro or age-grouper. I try to avoid what I did at Kona in 2009 when I was on my feet in the hot sun for an hour two days before the event for a hastily scheduled sponsor obligation. My coach, at the time, wasn't too happy...

As you can see, proper planning is very important to me and I do think it is one of many factors that allows me to race consistently. If possible, I avoid everyday tasks, like driving, to keep the stress meter at low. Aaron insists on driving me to all my workouts, sponsor obligations, and events during race week, thus making it one less thing I have to think about; traveling, whether via car or plane, often leads to anxiety. I study my race packet on the flight, which gives me the advantage of knowing what to expect when I arrive. The elevation of the course, layout of the race, and understanding of specific rules of each race becomes knowledge that I have about the event, which will subconsciously make me more confident. This is exactly like the public speaker reviewing notes before a speaking engagement.

Another important scheduling task is taking care of your bike—a cause for concern for every racer. I am not a mechanical wizard, so it is a must for me to have someone whose core competency is repairing bikes to look at mine prior to racing. A few weeks before each race, I determine if I know a competent mechanic heading to the event, or if I know individuals at the local bike shop. One of my go-to mechanics is Jeff Yingling based out of Boulder, Colorado. He is one of the best gearheads out there who has discovered many problems with my setup and efficiently corrected them. He is a trusted resource I can bounce ideas off of, and I am always confident riding after he has thoroughly inspected my machine. I also trust Nick Nicastro of Sag Monkey, who has developed a business around bike tune ups on site at major races and recently, bike guru Paul Buick or Darrell Koenig out of New Zealand.

I usually get my bike tuned at my local shop, Pacific Bicycle of San Francisco or City Cycle in Corte Madera. I then have them either box the bike for me or I take it to TriBike Transport in order to be transported intact to the race site. Once I arrive at the race, I immediately take my bike to either Jeff or Nick if they are on site, or I call the local bike shop to build up the bike and perform a final tune-up. I ride it once or twice on my race wheels to make sure everything is in order. If it is not, I work with the mechanic to diagnose the problem. After losing my bike seat during a race, I now always double-check the bike seat, the position of the XLAB hydration systems, the bike computer, and the components battery. I also double-check the Challenge Tires to make sure there aren't obvious abrasions after my trial cycling sessions. All of this preparation allows me to sleep better at night knowing I did everything I could to ensure the performance of the bike and all its parts. As triathletes, we know a lot can go wrong with the bike on race day, so take the steps to ensure you have confidence in your setup.

There are a few more small scheduling items you should think about and take care of before race week. If you are traveling internationally, make sure you update your cell phone plan to include the country where you are traveling. It may cost a few extra dollars, but it will save you the hassle of having disrupted service or excessive cellular fees.

You should also alert your credit card companies to avoid the hassle of having your card declined. You can usually take care of both of these items online.

Allocating Time

When you are planning your schedule for a race, always set aside time for relaxation and sleep. A nap, or multiple naps, of thirty minutes to three hours in the week before a race will help your body heal, clear your mind, and deflect mental fatigue. Relaxation can entail sitting in your Recovery Boots in your hotel room while vegetating in front of the TV. Activities where you are off your feet and not using too much brainpower are ideal. This includes turning off your computer and opting out of social media. These both require using your brain muscles, and even though you are sitting down, you are creating anxiety. The best prepared I have ever felt for a race was before Ironman New Zealand 2012. It was just my husband and I in a hotel room in Taupo, New Zealand, for a week. It was raining a lot of the time, so we just relaxed in the hotel after my morning workouts, concentrating on nutrition and hydration and watching every movie on HBO. It was simple, relatively stress-free, relaxing, and enjoyable. I know this can't happen before every race, but if you are able to do it once, why not strive for this feeling at other events?

I detailed my schedule before Oceanside 70.3 in 2012 to give you an example of what most pros try to accomplish before an event. The details are not as elaborate as a full Ironman, however, you can see the obligations and preparation it takes in order to travel, intake of proper hydration and nutrition, register, and compete in a race. I kept to the high-level concepts and started on the travel day; as you know, preparation begins many weeks before.

Thursday, March 29th

- 7:30 a.m.—Breakfast of Jeri Howlands Bungalow Munch granola, yogurt, banana
- 8:00 a.m.—Run and swim in morning, per my workout plan—fuel during workout
- 10:00 a.m.—Take supplements; hydrate; drink protein shake

- 10:15 a.m.—Drive to airport; use coupon for free day to reduce parking cost
- 11:15 a.m.—Eat healthy burrito at airport
- 11:50 a.m.—Fly direct to San Diego—bike and gear bag on TriBike Transport because checked luggage costs $50 each way
- 1:30 p.m.—Arrive in San Diego; pick up rental car
- 2:30 p.m.—Drive straight to race; check in before crowds arrive
- 3:30 p.m.—Get bike and gear bag at TriBike Transport; bring bike to mechanic to have it checked and tuned
- 4:30 p.m.—Meet with sponsors for pictures and fan greeting
- 5:45 p.m.—Check in at hotel; drop off clothes and gear
- 6:45 p.m.—Attend Ironman CEO Challenge dinner; mingle with patrons; eat healthy meal of salmon, mashed potatoes, sushi with brown rice, and sparkling water
- 8:30 p.m.—Head back to hotel; return emails; update social media
- 10:00 p.m.—Set up race bags; fill water bottles; prepare gear for race
- 11:00 p.m.—Sleep with white noise machine

Friday, March 30th

- 7:40 a.m.—Wake up after good night's sleep
- 8:00 a.m.—Breakfast of Van's gluten-free waffles, Nutella, banana
- 8:45 a.m.—One-hour run; ninety-minute ride to check bike performance; fuel and hydrate properly during workouts
- 11:30 a.m.—Thirty-minute swim to shake everything out
- 12:00 p.m.—Lunch of eggs, potatoes, protein shake, and gluten-free toast
- 1:00 p.m.—Meetings with sponsors Xlab and Rudy Project; discussion with Julia Polloreno, editor-in-chief of *Triathlete Magazine*
- 3:00 p.m.—Pro-panel presentation; answer questions from fans
- 3:30 p.m.—Drop off run bag at Transition 2

- 4:00 p.m.—Attend pro meeting to discuss race rules and course
- 4:30 p.m.—Drive to hotel; snack; use Recovery Boots
- 5:45 p.m.—Last gear preparations; water bottles in freezer
- 6:30 p.m.—Dinner with friends—chicken over rice; no vegetables
- 8:00 p.m.—Return emails; update social media use Recovery Boots; relax
- 10:00 p.m.—Sleep with white noise machine; sip hydrating drink throughout the night

Saturday, March 31st

- 4:00 a.m.—Wake up; shower; hydrate
- 4:30 a.m.—Breakfast of Van's gluten-free waffles, Nutella, banana
- 4:45 a.m.—Recovery Pump to loosen legs
- 5:00 a.m.—Drive to race site with bike; park near finish, conveniently accessible to Aaron so he can drive out on course to bring post-race bag and clothes
- 5:15 a.m.—Walk ten minutes to swim start and bike rack
- 5:45 a.m.—Fifteen-minute warm-up jog
- 6:20 a.m.—Put on wetsuit twenty minutes before start
- 6:40 a.m.—Race start
- 11:00 a.m.—Post-race interviews; drug testing
- 12:00 p.m.—Return to hotel; shower; pack; check out of hotel
- 1:30 p.m.—Lunch with friends—eggs, potatoes, toast, and protein shake
- 3:30 p.m.—Locate bike in transition; break down; give bike and gear bag to TriBike Transport
- 4:00 p.m.—Awards presentation
- 4:30 p.m.—Fulfill final sponsor obligations
- 5:30 p.m.—Head to airport
- 6:45 p.m.—Healthy burrito at airport
- 7:30 p.m.—Fly direct to San Francisco
- 9:30 p.m.—Arrive home
- 10:30 p.m.—Relax; use Recovery Boots and ice

- 12:00 a.m.—Sleep

Sunday, April 1st

- 9:30 a.m.—Wake up after sleeping in
- 9:45 a.m.—Breakfast of eggs and toast
- 10:30 a.m.—Ninety-minute swim to shake things out
- 12:30 p.m.—Brunch
- 2:00 p.m.—Back to regular routine

The point I want to emphasize is everything won't go exactly according to plan. However, I have prepared myself enough to make sure I am in a position to be race ready. Accomplishing all of my pre-race tasks requires being organized before the event, knowing where I am going at all times, remembering my nutrition and hydration, and eliminating unnecessary stress around race week by staying true to my routine. It has taken me awhile to learn how to say "No," but sometimes, in the interest of being of sound body and mind before a race, I have to avoid compromising my schedule. Athletes need to be wary of requests that throw off their finely tuned routines, including last-minute sponsor obligations. Once again, events will pop up out of your control, so adjust and keep your eyes on the prize: to have a fun, healthy race.

Pre-Race Workout Routine

I follow a specific workout routine a week before the race in order to keep the muscles moving. As I have mentioned before, a race is a small blip on my radar of building for a triathlon. I never taper leading into a race, but I also do not execute huge volume the week before. I try to listen to my body to determine if a shorter workout would be best. I write out a race-week workout, and I schedule the workouts around my other obligations. I like to get my workout completed early in the day to somewhat simulate the race time; this also lets me concentrate on hydration and nutrition for the remainder of the day. Remembering to fuel before, during, and after workouts is very important during race week because you want your muscles to perform the proper recovery.

I usually conduct my race-week swim workouts at a local pool. With online research it is relatively easy to find a community center or public pool located near the event, so I can get my swim workouts in with little interruption. I have never felt the need to swim the course, although I will study the venue in the race athlete guide, and I always visit the site to observe where the buoys are placed. The thought of gearing up in my wetsuit to swim the course in an unfamiliar body of water is not appealing to me. This is a personal preference. I know a lot of pros that like to swim the course, but you won't see me in the water until race morning.

Driving a small section of the bike course gives me a feel for its landscape. I don't necessarily drive the whole course because of time constraints or traffic, but checking out a ten-mile clip when possible gives me an idea of what to expect on the bike. This is the opportunity to take notice of the roughness of the pavement, if the sides are clean and swept, and the strength and direction of the wind. The pavement can be rough chip seal like you find in New Zealand or smooth asphalt like you find on the Ironman Arizona course. Obviously, with the chip seal, your tires will need to handle more wear and tear, and you will have to push more power because it provides more resistance. I also study the race guide to get a mental picture of the course, see if there are any unusual, sudden turns, and how much climbing is involved.

As a rule, I locate a gym near the race site to complete my run workouts on a treadmill. Once again, working out on a treadmill is my comfort zone; I would rather get on the machine and pound out my running than navigate the streets of a strange city. Although I am not opposed to running outside, I prefer running in a controlled environment. Like on the bike course, studying the race guide to get a mental image of the run course and taking note of the elevation gain is my way of making sure there will be no surprises on race day.

Steering clear of weight training and deep massages during race week are my keys to avoiding sore muscles. I step up my functional weight training during the off-season and when I have a long layoff between races. No one will suddenly get stronger during race week, so I try to make sure my muscles are in optimal condition going in, which means not stressing them with extra weight training. The stress on your muscles from a deep-tissue massage is the equivalent of a workout, and it is important to give yourself adequate time to recover from this. I may get a light massage before a race but definitely not a deep, full massage.

I have included sex in this section because, technically, it is a workout. I was intrigued by its relationship to athletic competition after hearing how some boxers, like Muhammad Ali, refrain from it months before their fights, believing it increases their aggression and athletic prowess. There have been studies on the subject, and the majority concluded there is no correlation between sex and athletic performance. Some athletes like to continue as usual because it calms their nerves and relaxes them, and others deprive themselves for fear they will be less energetic during their athletic event. Whatever stance you take, the end result should be that it will help you psychologically on race day; it won't affect your athletic output positively or negatively.

Laid out below is my average pre-race workout routine. This is what I do before a half- or full-distance Ironman, and I try not to deviate unless my body is telling me to decrease the volume for a particular reason, like if I feel a cold is coming on. I start the plan on Monday if the race is on Sunday. In this scenario, I am usually traveling to the race site on Thursday, so I do get to train in my own environment for the majority of the week. The workouts are done after breakfast in the morning, and my afternoons are usually free unless I have to teach a cycling class or my travel disrupts the schedule. I have learned that, for me, it is best to keep the engine open during race week and still put in the work.

Pre-Race Workout Routine
Monday
- Ninety-minute cycling class at an indoor facility
  o Aerobic builds in zones two and three
- Twenty-minute run off the bike
- Three to four thousand-yard "MBK-style" straight swim (back and forth, no stopping)
Tuesday
- Five thousand-yard early morning swim
  o Keep the engine open with a long warm-up
  o Fast hundreds, fifties, twenty-fives (yards)

- o Race-pace two hundreds
- o End with a long cool-down pulling
- Forty-minute easy run
- Teach ninety-minute cycling class at indoor facility in afternoon at zone two

Wednesday

- Three-hour double cycling class
  - o Twenty-minute warm-up
  - o Four minutes at threshold power with four minutes easy in-between six times
- Twenty-minute run off the bike
- Three to four thousand-yard easy swim
  - o Lots of pulling and band-only work (band around ankles)

Thursday

- Forty-five- to sixty-minute easy run
- Three thousand-yard easy swim

Friday

- Ninety-minute bike ride on the racecourse (if possible)
- Forty-four hundred-yard swim
  - o One thousand-yard warm-up swim
  - o Six hundred-yard sets with some effort four times
  - o One thousand-yard swim cool down

Saturday

- Sixty- to ninety-minute bike ride on the racecourse (if possible)
- Five minutes at race pace with plenty of recovery in-between four times

Sunday

- Race

Pre-Race and Race Day Mental Preparation

I usually try to keep the day before a race free of any firm commitments, although your business may require some appearances. It is important to follow your written plan for the day to give you the consistency you need before you race. For me, this means I rest, hang out with friends and family, use my Recovery Boots, and have a simple dinner. If at all possible, I try to have dinner at Outback Steakhouse because I can get my "before race meal" there. Everyone has traditions, and my pre-race-day dinner has developed into a basic meal with family and friends; I receive human interaction, enjoy a good meal, and calm my nerves.

As the pre-race hype wears down, it is just you and your thoughts the night before the race. I perform an exercise where I visualize the course, starting with the swim, all the way through the run sections of the triathlon. I cover the details, from my pre-race warm-up to breaking through the tape at the finish line. I envision the transition, and I mentally reexamine my bike setup and contents of my special-needs and run bags.

There have been multiple studies done on the positive effects of visualization and its influence on an athlete's performance. Although these studies have taken place for sports like basketball and golf, the same concepts should apply to triathlon. Visualize yourself in situations, and it will seem like you have been there when the real event occurs. This could be as simple as visualizing yourself putting on your running shoes in transition or as intense as mentally picturing yourself hammering the hills of the event. In both cases, you are using your down time to give yourself an extra edge on your competition.

The last step I take in my visualization process is to attach my favorite race songs to different sections of the course. I am a big believer that your body responds in a positive way to energized music, so why not hum some tunes on the course? It could be the motivational words or the beat, but certain songs keep my mind focused, push me physically to places I wouldn't normally go, and increase my enjoyment on the course. You have multiple hours to kill while you are racing, so why not add a little imaginative motivation?

Recently, I detailed my visualization and mental resilience techniques for an article written by Holly Bennett for *Triathlete Magazine*. The article provides additional examples of what to think about before and during races. Everyone has different motivation, so take my philosophy and tweak it to find *your* motivation.

"The Ball is the Finish Line" by Meredith Kessler
I firmly believe that triathlon is far more than just swim, bike, and run. Mental resilience is a crucial component of the sport, which requires precise visualization of how to "cope and rally" with all the peaks and valleys that happen before, during, and even after a race.

Growing up playing ample team sports, and as a collegiate Division I field hockey player, it was always ingrained in my head to anticipate the needs (of your teammates) on the field and *always* keep your eye on the ball. I was constantly envisioning a potential assist, an aspiring goal, or how to make a proper tackle when on defense—before they even happened.

This team sport mentality parlayed into triathlon for me, as I use the same visualization strategies I did back then, now—daily. In triathlon, the ball *is* the finish line.

It is helpful to go over the "play by plays" of the race in your head in order to keep everything dialed in. It's important to picture yourself swimming in open water and rallying through potential swells, keeping relaxed on the bike in aero position, while hydrating and fueling, and then going through the same motions on the run, while keeping your eye on the end goal—the finish line.

While the team component is a little different in triathlon, my TEAM now may not be ten other players on the field, but instead (my team) consists of my husband, coach, sponsors, family, and friends in this capacity. In both training and racing, I visualize my "TEAM" wherever they may be—cheering and smiling from afar—or I picture where they will be on the course, their happy faces, especially at the finish line, and how much I really love them all and appreciate their support.

I picture my best friend's little ones sitting at the computer on race day watching "Auntie Mer" on their screens and wondering why on earth she is wearing a seal suit or has on a pointy helmet! I think about the videos and pictures they will send me of this post race. Throughout both training and racing, I am constantly reminded how lucky I am to

149

have people who care so much about this journey. Channeling all of these thoughts is what fuels me to the finish every time.

As triathletes, I think we all need to visualize the finish line in all its glory, after all, how else are we going to get there? It's always a pleasant sight and it brings all the things we have envisioned *together*.

In addition to the above strategy, like most of us, I'm very inspired by music while training. During these music-blaring sessions, I especially picture my "TEAM" as mentioned above. We understandably do not have music during our races, so I usually go into the race with a handful of favorite tunes in my head. The musicality of those songs runs through my head during a race OVER and OVER and OVER, and they remind me of both good and bad training days when that particular music was playing, thus giving me extra momentum. End

*

Pre-Race and Race Day Nutrition and Fueling

I diagramed what I ate during a "normal" week and a race week in the "Nutrition, Hydration, Fueling, and Recovery" chapter. I wanted to use this section to take a higher-level view of my pre-race and race-day nutrition, as well as to look at what I consume during a half- and a full-distance Ironman. Once again, everyone is different. I will need a lot less fluid and calories before and during a race than a two hundred-pound age-group male. All pros will tell you they have their own quirks and a "go-to meal" before a race, no matter how unusual. Some athletes claim they have a few glasses of wine to calm their nerves. Not too much changes between my regular and race-week diet, but there are a few specific details I concentrate on to ensure I toe the line in optimal condition.

It is easy to become preoccupied with the hoopla surrounding race week, so the important tasks of eating and drinking can slip your mind on occasion. A water bottle, protein bars, and snacks are in my backpack at all times as I travel to my pre-race obligations.

There are a few foods I do not consume during race week because of the effect they may have on my body. I stopped drinking caffeine at the beginning of 2012, and this is heightened during race week, as I avoid all caffeine until the run where I drink Red Bull and eat caffeinated gels. I have eased up on this in recent years but I still monitor caffeine intake. I also avoid gluten and vegetables the majority of race week, but I really clamp down two to three days prior to the event. I struggled in a lot of triathlons with stomach issues, as a lot of triathletes seem to do, so I researched and tweaked to find the culprit. I realized that gluten and vegetables put unneeded stress on my stomach and they provided little benefit for the actual race. The solution was to eliminate them. To be clear, I am not allergic to gluten, but I concluded I could live without it around the race. As a result of a rising awareness of the disruptive effects of gluten on many people's stomachs, there are many gluten-free options readily available, so adhering to this rule is not an issue. Although the health benefits of vegetables are undeniable, they wreak havoc on my stomach during a race. On race day, trips to the Porta-Potty are inevitable if they are in my system.

Although there might not be a direct correlation with any particular ailments, there are a few other items I tend to stay away from to reduce the odds that something horrible will happen to my stomach. I do not eat sushi or raw fish during race week for fear of eating a bad batch, which would leave me reeling before the event. Food-borne illness is not something to mess around with. I do what I can to make sure all the food I eat is thoroughly cooked. I am also inclined to drink bottled beverages during race week, especially when in foreign countries. Although the water is probably perfectly fine, your stomach might not be used to the particular infectious agents located in the country or the region's tap water. I often bring bottled water to eating establishments as well. It is important I ingest liquids and foods my body is used to because I do follow the rule to not try anything new during race week. There are definitely going to be times where it is impossible to adhere to these rules, but the name of the game is to lessen the chances of developing some sickness before the race.

I eat at least two bananas per day two weeks before my race to supply my body with potassium. Since high school I have been taught that bananas help against cramping, and I have stuck to this regimen during my endurance sports career. They supply the potassium needed to regulate body water, help with muscle contractions, and aid in your body's recovery. I buy my bananas green because I do not like any type of bruising. I eat them almost every morning and maybe one as a snack in the afternoon.

The night before a race, I wear my Recovery Boots as I wait to fall asleep. I make sure that I am hydrated by monitoring the color of my urine, and I keep a sixteen-ounce hydrating protein drink on my nightstand to sip throughout the night to make sure I am hydrated eight hours later for the start of the race. I usually go to the bathroom a few times during the night. I do not take a sleeping aid the night before a race because my rest is usually interrupted with having to go to the bathroom, drinking, and the excited anticipation of the race. If you plan on catching up on sleep the night before a race forget it. It just doesn't happen. If you come into the final day tired, it will show in your performance, no matter how much sleep you get the night before.

On the way to the swim start, I consume three individual blocks and drink some additional water to aid in the digestion of the blocks. A general rule is you need sixty ounces of water to help digest five hundred calories or twelve ounces for one hundred calories. Once on the bike, it is imperative to fill your water bottles at the aid stations or you will not be able to properly digest the calories you are consuming, which will hurt you in the run. Carrying all your water with you on the bike is not possible in a full Ironman, consequently, you have to make yourself slow down and fill up to maximize your chances of finishing the race strong. I also consume enough BASE Electrolyte Salt to maintain a good balance in my body. I have been in situations where I did not consume electrolytes, and the results were not pretty.

The fueling and hydration on the run is a lot less regimented than the pre swim and bike. I operate more on feel than anything else, but I still have to ingest the necessary calories to keep motoring along. In addition to solid fueling, I have a sixteen-ounce bottle of a hydrating protein drink in my run transition bag, and I sip on this through the first few miles of the run. I then grab a cup of water at every aid station. As mile ten rolls around in a Half Ironman, or mile thirteen in a full, if I am feeling sluggish, I switch to Red Bull, which is now provided on some racecourses. If I am feeling any abnormal pain, I take one or two ibuprofen around mile seven of the run; at this point, the ibuprofen will not hurt my hydration (prolonged use before an event can cause dehydration during the race) in a full or half Ironman but will help dull pain. The result is I consume about 125 calories per hour, all the water I can get my hands on, controlled amounts of Red Bull, electrolyte salt, and ibuprofen.

There are a few things to be careful of when planning your nutrition and fueling for a race. When eating breakfast, the goal is to eat the proper nutrition but not overload the stomach before the events of the day. As always, never do anything new on race day that you have not practiced before. Do not try gels for the first time or switch to eating real potatoes when you haven't done your due diligence on how your body will react to them. There is a high probability your stomach and body will not be pleased with the new foods. Hydrating drinks are great to a degree, but water is what the body needs and craves. Be careful to monitor the ingredients of these drinks because they can contain high amounts of sodium and fructose. The Gatorade you are consuming could be your worst enemy on a long day of racing, because it can possibly cause cramps or diarrhea. I am also careful with the amount of caffeine I consume around race day. Some people swear by the caffeine enriched gels before and throughout the race. I typically avoid them until I need a boost later on the bike or in the run. This also includes the caffeine in Red Bull. Once again, these are the substances that negatively affect *my* body so I have learned to adjust the intake to suit my needs; it is a delicate act on a fueling tight rope.

Below is a summary of my consumption for Ironman races in good conditions (what is consumed could change due to weather and other unforeseen factors).

70.3 Distance

- Pre race: Banana, two Van's gluten-free waffles, and Nutella, 500 calories; water, 48 ounces
- Pre swim: Three individual blocks, 100 calories; water, 12 ounces

- Bike: Two packs blocks, 400 calories; hydrating protein drink, 200 calories; water, 40 ounces or more; BASE Electrolyte Salt
- Bike Total Calories: 500–700
- Run: Vanilla gel, 100 calories; Double Espresso gel, 100 calories; hydrating protein drink, 180 calories; water, 32 ounces or more; flat Coke, 12 ounces; BASE Electrolyte Salt
- Run Total Calories: ~400 calories

Full Ironman Distance

- Pre race: Banana, two Van's gluten-free waffles, Nutella, protein drink, 600 calories; water, 48 ounces
- Pre swim: Three individual blocks, 100 calories; water, 12 ounces
- Bike, first five miles: Three individual blocks, 100 calories; BASE Electrolyte Salt
- Bike, top of hour, every hour: One pack blocks, 5 packs; BASE Electrolyte Salt
- Bike: Four packs blocks, 800 calories (I try to have 250–300 calories per hour); two bottles of hydrating protein drink, 180 calories each, 360 calories total; water, 60 ounces (20–24 ounces of liquid per block); BASE Electrolyte Salt right before exit bike
- Bike special-needs bag: One 16 ounce bottle of hydrating protein drink, may or may not consume, 180 calories
- Bike Total Calories: 1200–1500
- Run, transition: One bottle hydrating protein drink, 180 calories
- Run, every forty-five minutes: BASE Electrolyte Salt
- Run, mile one: Vanilla gel, 100 calories
- Run, mile four: Vanilla gel, 100 calories
- Run, mile seven: One ibuprofen
- Run, mile eight: Double Espresso gel, 100 calories
- Run, mile twelve: Double Espresso gel (if I can still eat at this point), 100 calories
- Run: Water, a cup from EVERY aid station; Red Bull, a cup from every other aid station after mile thirteen
- Run, special-needs bag: One bottle hydrating protein drink on back half of run, 180 calories

- **Run Total Calories: ~800 calories**

When it comes to pre-race and race-day nutrition, if it isn't broke, don't fix it. If you never had nutritional issues during a triathlon, why change your game plan? However, if you are perplexed by your stomach problems on the racecourse, take portions of my routine, practice them, and see if you notice improvement. You can then transfer these changes to your race-week routine with the confidence your body will react favorably to your new system. The changes to how you feel will not happen overnight, and it will take some experimentation to find your magical formula.

Sami Inkinen is an accomplished age-grouper, as well as co-founder of the company Trulia. As someone who has experienced debilitating stomach issues since childhood, he developed a system that allows him to race a full Ironman while avoiding his stomach problems. He is meticulous about his training and racing analysis, and I found his nutrition and fueling system fascinating. Although I do not follow all of his pre-race rituals, I am impressed with his determination to solve his intense stomach issues and share his information with others. His system does not apply to everyone, but it shows the persistence of a triathlete to solve his problems, race to his potential, and achieve his goals. The following is an excerpt from his blog.

Excerpt from "Liquid Diet—My secret to Iron Stomach in any endurance event" by Sami Inkinen (www.samiinkinen.com)

I am one of those unlucky people who has a very sensitive stomach. Give me a tiny bit milk, travel to a new time zone, sleep in a new environment, too much stress, or a slight change in diet, and my stomach is ALL messed up like Swiss clockwork, so I can sympathize with those people who I see running to a bush or Porta-Potty for number 2s or 1.5s during a marathon or triathlon…

No offense, that used to be me too, but I've perfected an approach to pre-race nutrition in order to avoid these GI issues, and I now have exactly ten years of bush-free half marathons, marathons, and (Ironman) triathlons—meaning, not a single stomach issue or run to a bathroom/bush/ditch during fifty or more two hour plus endurance events. Here's how:

My approach is based on two principles and assumptions:
Create a systematic *process* that is repeatable time after time once proven to work.
If there is *nothing* solid in your digestive system at the start line and you eat *nothing* solid during a race, it is unlikely that something other than pee and sweat comes out of you.
The result is what my wife calls the patent-pending **Sami Liquid Diet**, which can be summed up in one sentence: From twenty hours before the start until you cross the finish line, only eat liquids.

Really.
In more detail, this is the process that I use:

T-2 days:
· Normal eating plus carb loading to fill up glycogen stores using the more recent scientific evidence…
T-1 days:
· **Breakfast:** Fiber-heavy clean food (e.g. apple, oatmeal, rye bread, etc.), about 500–800kcal.
· **Pre-race workout:** 200-400kcal liquid carbohydrates to fuel most of carb losses.
· **Post-workout meal (by 10 a.m. or so):** Fiber-heavy clean food (e.g. oatmeal, bread).
· **Rest of the day:** Strictly only liquids in about 25/25/50 percent ratio of fat/protein/carb by energy content. Potentially add some sodium to the drinks…
Race Day:
· **Immediately after waking up:** 10dl or more water, 50mg caffeine (that's about a cup of black tea), and some sodium (that's accessible e.g. in table salt)…
· **Race day breakfast (2–4 hrs before start):** 100kcal (25g) protein, 100kcal (10g) fat, 300kcal (75g) carbohydrates from fruit/veg juice and maltodextrin.
· **DURING last ninety minutes before start:** 200kcal (50g) carbohydrates from maltodextrin and fructose in a bike bottle (7.5dl)…
It goes without saying that this is based on my own ten years and fifty

plus races of experimentation, and I'm sharing this only as a thought and not taking any responsibility if this protocol screws up your A race! Of course it is possible to still create conditions for gas or pure water absorption in your digestive system, but that's a matter of race-time nutrition. Avoid eating or drinking too much fructose (a.k.a. fruit sugar) or drinking a gallon of seawater, for example.

*

The complete plan is on Sami's blog, so please check that out. Though it is not for everyone, it is very interesting.

Race Strategy

To the average spectator, the normal flow of a race does not reveal the triathlete's strategy behind each event. Athletes enter and exit the water for the swim, they zip by on the bike in a fleeting second, and, depending on the course, they can be cheered on a few times during the run. From the outside, the swim looks like a mad dash in water churning inside a washing machine. The only apparent strategy involves not getting kicked in the face and then finding an open lane to actually complete a stroke. During the bike, fans watch a whirlwind of athletes zoom by as they frantically try to figure out who is who, because everyone looks the same. During the run, with the slower pace, the spectator can give athletes more encouragement, and they probably will see an athlete drink some water or eat a gel along the way. Even then, the runners continue to fly past, striving for the finish line, and the strategy of this long event usually escapes the spectators. This perception is so far removed from the truth of what actually goes into an Ironman/triathlon event.

When I first began racing Ironmans, the goal was to finish the race, no matter how I did it. There was no concept of strategy, no preparation for nutrition and hydration, and no thought given to the other riders. This was my naivety in entering a new sport and not taking the proper steps to race smart and efficiently. As I worked to get better at the three disciplines, I began to take note of my surroundings during a race. This included realizing it was not the best strategy to just race as fast as my body could take me until I finished. I learned tactics from watching other athletes that helped me arrive at the finish line faster. When I turned pro, it became clear I would have to adopt more strategy and technique to compete with the elite triathletes. You could have all the talent in the world, but if you do not race with a plan, more experienced athletes will leave you in a cloud of dust.

Strategy does not necessarily mean executing tactical moves during an event. Strategy starts well before the actual race in preparing with your gear, knowing your competitors, and becoming familiar with the course. If you have these aspects of your racing dialed in, you will be more prepared than the majority of your competitors. Tom Brady does not go into a football game without a defined plan to try to outmaneuver the competition. The team studies game tape, reads scouting reports, and deciphers the strengths and weaknesses of the opposing team to gain an advantage. The players also make sure all their equipment is primed and ready to go for the game. Any flaw in a football pad, shoe, or helmet could result in a disastrous outcome. For instance, if the weather isn't monitored and they do not have the proper cleats for the game conditions, the players could slip on the field.

As you race against individuals over time, you start to get a feel for their strengths and their weaknesses. In triathlon, an athlete has things he or she does well in each of the disciplines, just like a basketball player has certain tendencies, such as being a good rebounder, dribbling strong to the left, or consistently hitting shots from the top of the key. From race to race, you normally won't see huge improvements in one triathlete's ability; it is usually a steady increase in seconds or minutes off the race time that shows a change in preparation. This awareness will help you know what to expect going into a race with your competition. You also have useful services such as Thorsten Radde's www.trirating.com where you can look at prior results from your competition. You can track their improvement and easily see their strengths based on the course, which is valuable information to prevent you from racing "blind." You can know who to look for in the swim because their times are similar to yours or which athletes you need to be wary of on the run because they are hunting you down. Anything can happen during a race, but it is good to know the general tendencies of your competitors on race day.

Equipment, especially the bike, has been a pain point for me for years. You have to understand your equipment like the back of your hand to optimize your performance. It took me awhile to learn this, and it became my priority to increase my bike knowledge when I turned pro. Being uncomfortable with your gear will take minutes off of your time. It should be an extension of your body, like a baseball player and his glove. A golfer does not randomly pick a set of clubs each time he or she goes out golfing; it takes many years to dial in exactly what is needed based on your swing and golf course conditions. I have observed many triathletes, including myself, who do not take the time to figure out what works best for them in each of the three disciplines. It makes for an uncomfortable race, especially when you don't trust what you are using. If you don't think this all blends into race day strategy, think again. Part of race strategy is toeing the line with the optimal equipment that is specially designed for you.

In an ideal world, you would be able to blind test each wetsuit on the market by time trialing for two hundred meters, with no regard for brand or price. Each individual has a unique swimming style, and certain wetsuits work well with an individual's stroke. Some wetsuits have more padding to hold up the legs or around the torso, which may restrict movement in some individuals. I was a wetsuit agnostic for the majority of my amateur and pro careers, using what was convenient or in my price range. I have since learned wetsuits make a difference and the discrepancies can be dramatic for certain swimmers. I did a lot of research before choosing my current wetsuit partner, ROKA Sports, and their patent-pending design has proven tremendous for pros as well as middle of the pack age-groupers. The neoprene is strategically positioned to not restrict movement and keep the core temperature stable. Not everyone has the ability to experiment with multiple wetsuits, but choosing the right one will put you at a distinct advantage on race day.

I did not grow up around bikes, and the inner workings of the machine are like a foreign language to me. I have learned, through multiple races as an amateur and pro, if you do not have your bike tuned up before your race, you can lose minutes off of your overall time. This can be the difference between a podium or Kona slot and nothing, so having your bike on point is a huge part of race day strategy. Bike preparation includes using the correct components for the course, having the proper chain ring for your riding style, and optimizing the aerodynamics of your storage containers, bike computers, helmet, and positioning.

I talk a lot in this manual about bike fit, but aerodynamics and drag are also extremely important factors for that segment. I have recognized my shortcomings on the bike, so I have sought out and partnered with companies that can make me faster. These partnerships are part of my race day strategy. I am working with Xlab-USA to minimize the drag created by my storage units including bento box, water containers, and computer placement. I am also working with Atomic High Performance to reduce the drag with their coatings and lubricant created by the pedals, wheels, cassette, wheel jockeys, and chain rings. Rudy Project and I are trying to optimize my helmet for aero as well as ventilation. Companies like Ceramic Speed become your best friend; a silent assassin for 'free speed'!

You are on the bike the longest during a triathlon, consequently, it is necessary to make sure to reduce drag as much as possible and optimize the watts you are producing. I had a big problem with non-slick components and improperly placed storage units, which slowed me down. My positioning was upright, looking a mile ahead down the road, when I should have been more crouched over, with my head down, watching ten meters ahead of my front tire. Wind tunnel testing can expose these problems, but if you don't have that option, you should take the steps to obtain and tweak your gear to put you in the best position to be faster. Over the course of a five-hour, Ironman-distance bike, these small things add up and can hurt your legs for the run if not properly implemented. Eliminating a watt drag in multiple places will ultimately improve your overall triathlon time.

Components add weight to the bike, which increases drag, so it is best to find the ones that are efficient and reduce weight but allow you to maximize your watt output. I researched chains, cassettes, chain rings, brakes, and wheel jockeys to figure out the correct combinations going into a race based on the course. I am partial to the Shimano Di2 system, which is electronic shifting. Once you go from mechanical to electronic shifting, it is tough to go back because this is one less thing to worry about during the event. The course will determine the cassette you use because one that helps you on the hills might not be right for a flat and fast race. The optimal length of chain is determined by your cadence and wattage. If you are spinning on the highest gear, you are not maximizing your output; this could mean the chain or length of crank is a problem. At the very least, you need to understand your components by doing your due diligence and researching or picking the brain of a qualified bike technician. Even if you just get a high-end overview, you will be much more aware than before and it will ultimately help you in your racing.

Wheels come in all styles and sizes, and it is important to figure out which ones are best for you and then practice on them. The wind conditions will ultimately determine the size of the wheels you use. On a particularly windy day, I use a shallower front wheel to minimize the effects of the sideways blasts of wind. When a strong wind is coming from the side, it is much better to be pushing a big gear, and when the gust hits the bike, you want to put more tension on the chain. This creates a linear force to counteract the lateral force of the wind. The last action to do is pause, which creates an addition of pressure, and then push into the wind. If the wind is coming left to right, hitting on the left side, lean onto the bars and put slightly more weight on the wind side. This puts the wheels into the wind. You can read about riding technique, but the best teaching tool is getting out there and experimenting in adverse conditions. The techniques you learn will help you be faster and stay safe while riding.

The pieces of equipment to focus on for the run are your shoes and race belt. I don't have to tell you how important shoes are to your performance. You have to limit the pain and blisters on your feet, or you will be in for one uncomfortable race. The bottom line is that you have to pick a shoe that fits your feet correctly. Some brands are made wide or narrow and others may have pressure points at unusual spots on your feet. Experiment with different brands and make sure you try them out before you race. Saucony has been the ideal shoe for me in my triathlon career even though I grew up racing in Nike shoes. I use the T1 Pro Race Belt, which holds my gels, electrolyte salt, and race number. It is necessary to have a storage system to hold these items on the run or you won't be able to intake the proper nutrition.

I will admit this is easier said than done, but stay away from sick people leading up to and during race week, especially when consuming food. Nothing is more deflating than heading into race week and suddenly getting a tickle in your throat two days prior to the race. There is a lot going on mentally and physically before a race, so sometimes your body can be more susceptible to germs. I carry some sort of hand sanitizer in my purse and car at all times before an event. After sponsor obligations, fan meet and greets, and especially before eating, I wash my hands. This includes when I am eating blocks while working out in the morning. I make sure my hands are clean before ingesting the product. I love kids, but I am conscience of how much interaction I have with them around race week because of the potential for germs, although this doesn't always stop me! The plane ride is a Petri dish at thirty thousand feet, so I always overload on Vitamin C flying to races, and I am constantly washing my hands. This may seem a little paranoid, but triathlon is my job and it is not productive to show up on race day with a cold. Sickness weakens even the strongest of competitors.

The paragraphs above explain what is necessary to complete *before* race day in order to gain a strategic advantage. What's next? Game day strategy, of course—from the time you wake up until you cross the finish line. This is an overview on the inner workings of race strategy and what you can do to gain an advantage, make sure you finish the race, and improve your overall times.

Before going to bed, I have my transition and special-needs bags assembled, so all I have to do in the morning is put the frozen water bottles into them and leave for the race. My pump is also a necessary pre race item so that I do not have to scramble around to locate one to make sure the bike tires are fully inflated. I always set multiple alarms for two and a half hours before the start of the race, which allows me enough time to properly prepare for the day's endeavor. One of a racer's fears is to not wake up in time for the race, and I have seen many people sprinting to the swim and leaping into the wrong heat because they overslept. The first thing I do after I wake up is take a long shower. This gives me time to relax, visualize the activities for the day, and clear my head. In the shower I gulp my hydrating drink to maintain hydration or make up for the night's less frequent drinking and peeing. After showering I eat my race-day breakfast.

Hopefully, either after my initial breakfast in the hotel or before the ingestion of pre-swim blocks at the race site, I will be able to have a bowel movement. Here, the key is to get the proper nutrition before a race and also rid yourself of any unnecessary waste. A common site at all triathlons is long lines at the Porta-Pottys, which means most everyone is in the same boat—trying to rid themselves of excess water and excrement. It is ideal if I am able to handle this in my hotel bathroom an hour or two before the race, but it is inevitable to have races when it comes down to the last few minutes. Not being able "to go" before the race is not a deal breaker, but it will make for a more comfortable race, and I won't lose time in the Porta-Potty.

I give myself enough time for a warm-up run before the race and find strategically placed bathrooms so I can avoid waiting in the huge lines that inevitably form. One tip is to have a member of your crew stand in the long Porta-Potty line before the race while you warm up so you do not have to endure standing for ten minutes or more. Yes, I have seen lines longer than this. The last thing before the race is I apply the glide for the pressure points around the neck and ankles of the wetsuit to prevent rubbing.

As with any swim start, you have to study the course to know where you are going. It is imperative to know the fastest line between the buoys because directly following them might not be the shortest distance. You should also recognize how hard it is to see where you are going with the huge mass of people surrounding you, your low profile in the water, and few landmarks where you can gauge positioning. Do seek out individuals who you know are near your speed in the water. If you are in the lead pack, find those individuals as a pacing mechanism and to benefit from others breaking the water. Drafting is legal in swimming, so utilize it if possible, but don't be afraid to swim solo. It is tough to recover if you end up in a pack below your skill level, so concentrate on getting out to where you are comfortable and find others who are keeping the same pace. Recognize if your pack is drifting off the optimal course, as valuable minutes can be lost by taking a bad line.

Always bring both your wetsuit and skinsuit to the event just in case something drastic changes in the weather, resulting in a suit change. A rule of thumb is to wear what your competition is wearing because you do not want to give up any advantage that a wetsuit can provide. The speed a wetsuit presents over a skinsuit is well documented; so even if the water temperature is near where a skinsuit would be used, don't give up the wetsuit because the speed sacrificed is difficult to overcome.

Different course conditions will affect your overall swim strategy. You have to take in account the current, especially in an ocean or river swim. It is smart to know which way the current is flowing so you can adjust your start and swim direction. I have seen ocean swims where the current pushes the athletes fifty yards or more to the right or left, so you have to adjust your start to accommodate this movement. It takes a lot of energy to combat a current and time is sacrificed. If you are entering into swells, it is best to dolphin dive into the breaking waves to push yourself through the surf. You also have to know in what direction you are going around the buoys—if they will be on your right shoulder or left. International races sometimes go in a different direction than the ones in the United States.

My transition times have been traditionally slower than my competition, however, I have been working to improve this aspect of my racing. If you want to learn how to do a fast transition, study the Olympic distance and ITU pros; in those races, every second counts. Examine how far you have to run from the swim to the first transition (T1) and then how far you have to run on your bike before you get out on the open road. This will factor into how you approach these sections of the course. I know it sounds tedious and maybe a little odd, but practicing transitions is how you get faster at them.

In T1, you get out of your wetsuit and into your bike gear, but taking off your wetsuit quickly and efficiently is tough. The suit sticks to your body and does not slide off without a lot of effort. There are some races where volunteers help pull it off of you, but the majority of the time it is up to you to wiggle free from the confines of a wet, sticky suit. Hopefully, you set up your bike before the race, so all you have to do is jump on it and go. A lot of pros keep their shoes on the bike and maneuver them onto their feet when they first start riding. I do this sometimes if the course dictates this technique. With all things being equal, the best approach for me has been to put my shoes on in T1 and then immediately click in when I mount the bike. I usually end up catching the individuals who are still fiddling with their shoes while riding, so the time saved by keeping my shoes on the bike seems minimal. For longer races, I wear socks for the comfort. If it is a shorter race, I ride with no socks.

The swim is my "comfort zone" event, and I always try to stay with the lead pack for as long as I can hold the pace. It is imperative I get out of T1 as soon as possible to not lose sight of any cyclists in front of me and to put distance on the ones I know will be hunting me down. Obviously you want to study the course to recognize where the long sections are for hydrating and eating. You also want to be cognizant of the technical portions of the course. Staying alert is paramount in these areas so as to not put yourself in harm's way and to be able to successfully navigate them without taking a wrong turn. There are always races where people take a wrong turn on the bike, no matter how well it is marked, so you have to pay attention to these details.

Drafting on the bike is a hot topic in triathlon and non-drafting racing. If you bring it up to triathletes, the passion is evident. No one wants to be labeled as a drafter. In reality, drafting provides a huge advantage to the rider because less energy is utilized to produce the same amount of power, ultimately leading to a faster bike time. Also, the individual's legs are saved for the run. It has an enormous benefit, which makes it such a controversial subject for age-groupers and pros. The legal distance you need to be from another rider is twelve meters, but in some countries, like New Zealand, the distance is seven meters. If you pass another rider too slowly, or if the rider being passed does not drop back to the required distance fast enough, you will be penalized and have to spend multiple minutes in the penalty box.

The tough part about determining drafting is that while the judges who rule on riders' actions are sporadically spaced on the course, the number of riders and the length of the course create trouble with enforcement. An indication but imperfect sign of drafting is close spacing of competitors throughout sections of the course. Their proximity to one another is evidenced by their times or by catching up to the lead packs quickly through the ranks of the age-groupers. Pros and age-groupers who are slower swimmers do have to wade through scores of cyclists to try to catch up, and sometimes it is tough to maintain a draft-legal status in these sections of the race. The fact is, you cannot control what other riders do, so you shouldn't waste time worrying about it. You can be draft-legal and still gain an advantage from reduction of drag, so concentrate on being in the proper aero position in a draft-legal slot to help with your race.

As with swimming, if at all possible, locate cyclists that are equal or better than you and try to keep up while remaining draft-legal. You need to be pushed to achieve faster times, and your competition is who can do it. In most triathlon events, you will be racing with males and females among all age groups and pros on different portions of the course. Knowing this, you should be able to locate someone with your same skill level. A competitor can become an ally when pacing each other legally, and you can take comfort in having a newfound partner. You both can work to attack the sections, and you have another set of eyes to help avoid potential dangers. Another must for me is to use my PowerTap computer to keep track of my watts. I monitor my watts throughout the race to make sure I do not dip below my levels. I also make sure, if a competitor passes me, I do not blow my legs up trying to maintain the pace to keep up. You will be useless on the run if you crushed your legs trying to stay with a stronger cyclist.

If you know your ideal wattage output, then race your race, no matter what is going on around you. Keep your concentration, pay attention to the course and rely on a smooth cadence to propel you to the second transition (T2). Many riders will pull a bully tactic and try to speed by you with a tremendous amount of watt output. Their goal is to intimidate so other riders back down so that they consequently gain some distance on them. If it is in the beginning to three quarters of the way through the bike, I do try to keep up because no one can hold that high of watts for the rest of the race; short outbursts are part of racing. I am better at going up hills than going downhill, so I try to make up distance on these sections of the bike because I know other riders will speed by me when going downhill. Know your strengths and utilize them to your advantage on the ride.

Staying in the aero position will reduce your drag accordingly, so force yourself to stay in this stance as long as you can. You will need to stretch your back occasionally, especially on the long and flat bike courses. Being in the same position multiple hours can wreak havoc on those muscles used to stay in aero, and stretching will keep your back from locking up later in the ride and on the run. Also, don't be afraid to be vocal while riding, alerting athletes of your whereabouts and letting them know you are coming. Lastly, with all of your concentration focused on staying in aero, racing strategically, and being safe, do not forget to hydrate, eat, and ingest electrolytes on the bike. At this point in the race you are only a portion of the way up the mountain, and you won't see the top if you forget to take care of your body's energy and hydration needs.

After the bike you head into T2, and like T1, this transition should be practiced. It is crucial to figure out how your body reacts to being on the bike saddle for a long period and then jumping into a long run. My training regimen has multiple bike to run sessions during the course of the week, so my muscles will be used to this important action on race day. Speed is the key in transition; however, if your feet are not properly fitted into your shoes before you begin your run it will be detrimental later. Also, T2 is where you can pick up an extra water bottle and more fuel—do not forget your nutrition and hydration. I store my nutrition in the race belt and have a special hand-fitted water bottle or, on hot days, I put an extra bottle between my chest and race kit.

If you are behind the leaders, it is natural to try to make up as much distance as possible at the beginning of the run, but this can be a losing strategy. Use a watch and check your mile splits, slowly building up to your triathlon pace, depending on the distance. Keep track of your miles completed, because you want to make sure you pace yourself through the finish line. I have seen it happen way too often where athletes sprint to make up time and then crash out during the final miles. Don't be afraid to walk the aid stations to make sure you properly hydrate, although I tend to only slow down to a jog and avoid walking to avoid giving my body the wrong impression. Also, don't be afraid to pee on the course, whether it is in your wetsuit, on the bike, or during the run. You may need to practice this to get comfortable doing it; time spent in the Porta-Potty is time lost on your overall race. However, be cognizant of the race course rules because going the bathroom out in the open is illegal in most towns and can result in a penalty or worse. To me, a bowel movement is a different story. I suggest that if you don't want an extremely uncomfortable race, you should locate a Porta-Potty.

If you are being hunted on the run, relax and run your race. It is understandable to run scared, yet even if you know faster runners are chasing you, anything can happen during an event, so stay your course and don't panic. Don't clench your fists when you run; pretend you are carrying an egg, and this will allow you to keep a more relaxed running form. It is helpful for your crew to give you splits, but sometimes this is not possible on particular courses. Understand that not every split you hear from the crowd will be accurate. They might be way off base, so try to get data points from trusted sources. You are racing against your body, the course, and, finally, the rest of the field. Take care of the things you can control and then worry about the competition. A triathlon is survival all the way to the very end.

Hopefully, your hard work and smart racing pay off and you end up with a podium finish. This means your nutrition and hydration were spot on, you avoided stomach problems and did not start puking, and surprise bathroom breaks did not happen or were kept to a minimum. When you cross the finish line, avoid being draped by anything. Your sponsors paid good money to share in a finish line moment, so let your kit, and hopefully your smile, shine!

Post-Race Routine

Unfortunately, the day is not over when you cross the finish line. I equate it to climbing a mountain. When you experience the jubilation of reaching the peak and the glory that comes with it, the first thing to do is ENJOY IT! Relish the experience and have fun at this moment— the climax of all your hard work. This is what you have been training and sacrificing for, so take it all in. After the feeling dies down, you realize you have to climb back down the mountain in order to safely end your journey, or you will not have successfully completed the task at hand, i.e., put yourself in the best position to do it again. Any slipup on the way down the mountain can be just as perilous as the climb upward. You have to be calculated and smart in your descent, and, if need be, rely on the help of others to conclude your journey intact.

Many athletes in a triathlon are there to push their bodies to the limit, whether it is to beat personal goals, win their age groups, or win the entire race. It is not a requirement, but it is strongly suggested that you have a support crew. These are the people who helped get you to the race with all of your gear in place, they are the ones who cheered relentlessly on the course for multiple hours, and they will be the ones to help you make it past the finish line and to your final destination in one piece.

To the athletes' support crews: the finish line is where your day hits its crucial moments; it is where you need to help the athlete and gear make it safely to the final destination.

As a member of the support crew, your first step is to gauge the condition of the athlete. There have been some races where afterwards I can go out to dinner, I have coherent conversations, and the only immediate effect is the extreme soreness from competing in a multi-hour athletic event. Those are the finishes I strive for, but even with the best-laid plans, I can end in the fetal position. Sometimes athletes end a race so discombobulated, all they want to do is lie down, and the thought of doing anything is nauseating. These are the times when the crew needs to step in and help the athlete down the mountain.

As a racer, your mind is not clicking properly, and the athlete in you does not want to concede to the medical tent, even though, that could be exactly what you need to recover in a more efficient manner. At the very least, the support crew has to gauge this and make the decision to head to a more relaxed place or steer the athlete toward the medical tent to receive IVs. Your body will thank you the next day even though your mind might be saying no.

If you finished in the top ten in a race, you may have to be ushered away into a secluded drug testing area. This happens right after the race, and an official shadows your every move until you complete the drug testing. Both amateur and pro athletes are now subject to drug testing depending on the race series, your finishing position, and random selection from this subset. I have sat for hours in a drug-testing chamber because I could not generate enough pee to satisfy the sample needed for detection. The room can be vile, as athletes are spilling out of all orifices because of the intensity of the race. I have sometimes not peed during the run for fear of sitting in drug testing for an extended period of time after a race. That is not how I want my day to end. It is a necessary part of the sport, but it is the last thing you want to do after competing at a high level for multiple hours.

As crew, after you are confident the athlete's immediate needs are taken care of and drug testing has been determined, it is time to gather the gear. In triathlons, the athlete usually receives a card that will enable a crew member to retrieve it—not just anyone can go in and request the personal things of the athlete. This process can take as long as an hour depending on the length of the race, the number of competitors, and the proficiency of volunteers to check out the equipment to the rightful owners. There are usually swim, run, and special-needs bags, as well as the bike. These are obviously important items to the athlete, so they should be located after the race to ensure a speedy exit from the site. If you use services like TriBike Transport, the bike can be dropped off. Otherwise it must be brought to the vehicle or hotel room along with the athlete's gear.

In an ideal race, I am able to cross the finish line, hydrate and fuel properly, gather my gear, and walk under my own power to our mode of transportation. In reality, I usually require help with all of these functions. I need someone to keep telling me to drink because I am not entirely coherent, and my crew has to remind me to eat, if at all possible, to get some nutrients back into my body. The car can be as far as a mile away from the race finish line, so getting there with all my gear is difficult even with the help of my support crew. If possible, it is best to have someone get the car and try to get close to pick the athlete up. An athlete driving a car to a hotel after a race is not recommended. I remember doing the Vineman Ironman in my twenties thinking I could drive up, do the race, and return sixty miles to San Francisco without any problem. I ended up pulling over and passing out for a couple of hours because I could not keep my eyes open.

For the spectators and crew: remember, you may see your athlete in a horrible condition. Do not be alarmed by what you may see. This could include incoherent talking, uncontrollable chattering, wobbly walking, intense puking, and uncontrollable defecating. Unfortunately, this is a consequence of the sport and the intense physical and mental activity that goes with it. The volunteers at the races do a great job of trying to recognize a potentially dangerous situation and taking the athlete to the medical tent. However, after the jubilation of finishing, symptoms may arise long after the completion of the event, so carefully monitor him or her. I remember falling down in my hotel room bathtub and not having the motor functions or frame of mind to stop my fall or move once I landed. I was in full race clothes with water pouring over my head. It is not pretty, and it is sometimes quite ugly, but this is the sport in which we love to compete.

Triathletes, when you plan your race, remember to include the aspects of climbing down the mountain, because the trauma that could unfold afterwards can be as devastating as during the race. This may sound dramatic, but I have had plenty of races where the pain directly after the race and the next day exceeds the actual event because of poor post-race planning. Preparation includes taking the proper steps to make sure my body recovers, I have a well-thought-out exit strategy from the site with my crew, and I can efficiently get to a place where I can relax. I thank my support crew of family and friends who attempt to accomplish this at all my races, through the good and bad times.

Speech

The culmination of your hard work and a race where your stars are aligned could propel you to a victory. While being the first to run through the tape at the finish line is an exhilarating feeling, it also assigns you the task of giving a speech at the awards ceremony. After some of the smaller races, this could be an impromptu minute-long speech right after the race, or it could be a speech in front of thousands of people at a banquet the day after the race. In both cases, you are representing your brand and sponsors, so make sure you put some thought into what you want to convey and whom you would like to thank.

There are many ways to write and deliver a speech, and everyone has a unique flare, which is part of the intrigue of a speech in general. The majority of the audience has limited contact with the athlete so they are anxious to learn a little bit more about this individual they may only know through social media. A person can hide behind the walls of cyberspace and develop a persona, but there is no hiding when giving a speech, so it is best to prepare ahead of time. You never know when you may be thrust into the limelight in front of hundreds of fans after the race of your life.

I am not an English teacher, so you won't be getting pointers from me on how to prepare and write your speech, but there are a few things I can recommend *mentioning* or you may regret leaving them out when the moment has passed. Try to thank the race directors, volunteers, and your crew. The race could not happen without the tireless work of the race directors, and the volunteers are an absolute necessity for the success of any triathlon. If you have ever raced in a triathlon where volunteer support is lacking, you have seen how it severely hurts the overall success of the event. I am sure it can seem like a thankless job, and this is why it is so important for every finisher to try and express gratitude to the volunteers for all that they do.

You do not want to forget mentioning the individuals who helped you along the way. Triathlon is tough for the athletes as well as their supporters. There are a lot of duties your support crew has to perform in order for you to toe the line in the best possible position to have a quality race. There is also the fun task of cheering, and then the role of gathering equipment and providing transportation following the race. In the heat of the moment, your mind is racing, and you may overlook people you should thank, so take the time to remember to do this at the beginning or the end of your speech. To this day, I still remember the individuals I accidentally forgot to mention, and it still bothers me that I will never get that moment back to properly thank them.

The moral is, if you are fortunate enough to give a race victory speech, prepare to the best of your abilities and have no regrets after giving it. Do not make it a promotion fest, but do thank your influential sponsors who helped get you to the podium and try to incorporate your brand. Speak from the heart, and your personality will shine through. The audience will be able to recognize a genuine speaker no matter the manner of your delivery because not everyone is a flawless orator. Do remember your audience, which consists of families and individuals who have a true respect for your abilities, so refrain from offensive or negative tones. This is not the time. It is refreshing to hear a humble speech after an event where so many people came together to create a wonderful experience for the athletes and fans.

I have included my notes from my victory speech given at Ironman New Zealand 2016. I distinctly remember not being able to sleep the night after the race because my body was so out of whack from pushing its physical and mental limits. Although the actual speech is a blur, the written notes do capture the general theme.

Notes written for Ironman New Zealand speech 2016:
Thank you so much, Ironman New Zealand and the city of Taupo, for having us back to your precious town. This special place genuinely enriches our lives and continues to do so every time our toes touch the ground in New Zealand.

This week leading up to the race I had the opportunity to speak about the importance of the word GUMPTION at the Taupo Intermediate School and its meaning to me personally since I was a youngster. I said that GUMPTION has real meaning behind its punch. GUMPTION is what gets us up in the morning with the motivated mindset to pursue dreams (or simply our day) with fortitude and grace while accepting potential challenges, adversity and defeat. Most importantly, GUMPTION is about never letting anything break your stride or steal your light, emotionally, personally, and physically. What is so intriguing is that EVERY person who raced yesterday, regardless of your result, did it with GUMPTION and this is where the magic happens in life.

I'm a really big believer of CHI and ENERGY and where that lies in your spirit. We all have to channel our chi and energy toward things that matter to us personally. All of us, sitting here together tonight, have this special bond because we love the challenge of Ironman.

As 2016 approached, I became intent on everyone creating their new YOU 3.0; I recently learned that mindset from a good friend. Our YOU 1.0 is totally cool and manageable, maybe it has a little riff raff in it and likely a lot of things that need improvement. Hopefully, we eventually transition to our YOU 2.0 and we de-clutter a little bit more and strive to formulate some better methods in life and sport. We often and understandably can remain stagnant in our YOU 1.0 or 2.0 as life experiences tend to shift us up and down on this scale.

What we should all be aiming for is YOU 3.0, THE place to THRIVE. At YOU 3.0 we guard our hearts, we de-clutter the rest of the riff raff, and we accept that while we can't prevent negativity in life we do not have to allow it into our spirit.

In addition, with this new revitalizing YOU 3.0, we acknowledge that *we cannot control everything that happens to us.* That's BIG! But then we go a step forward and realize we can only control *the way we respond* to what happens and in that response is POWER! VERY LIBERATING POWER!

So, if you didn't think this American was sappy enough, now you know! I certainly do not claim to understand all the secrets to the world, but we can all agree there is a LOT of time to think during our sport and a chance to reflect on our individual experiences!

If you are wavering at all about your day yesterday and if it did NOT go as you envisioned, I think it's important to remember that we are stronger because of the hard times, wiser because of our mistakes, and happier because we have learned sadness, adversity, and stresses, both on and off the race course.

I would like to take a moment to reflect on the professional field. To the men's podium –

Callum Millward in 3rd - What is so great about you, Cal, is that while you are relentlessly fierce and strong ON the course, you are equally as funny, humble and down to earth off of it; what a terrific combination.

Joe Skipper in 2nd - Your pink hair, alone, set the tone for your amazing day; energetic, fierce, vibrant and fiery. Congratulations on your second place!

Cameron Brown in 1st - It is hard to say much that already hasn't been said about you. I actually Googled the word legend and it said it was an 'important or notorious person who is known for doing something extremely well in a particular field'. I would say that is you to an absolute tee! Congratulations on your 12th Ironman New Zealand title!

Congratulations gentleman! It was a fine day of racing.
To the ladies up here on this stage:

Vanessa Murray in 10th – Her 2nd race as a pro, having been 6th in her pro debut in January at Challenge Melbourne, is quite an achievement!

Candice Hammond in 9th – She already has a 2nd place this year at the Taurange Half Triathlon. This was just inside a year after having her son, Flynn. Impressive to say the least! Candice is always an athlete and now a mom that will prosper.

Gina Crawford in 8th - I have had the pleasure of racing with Gina over the years and continue to be in awe of all that she manages as a mother and professional triathlete and how she follows her passions. She is back in the orchestra playing the violin and now also a coach in our sport. Any athlete would be fortunate to work with Gina in this capacity. This gal has marquee experience of her craft and she knows what it takes to be a winner; I have lost count of how many full distance titles she has won.

Maureen Hufe in 7th - Mighty Maureen; She genuinely defines that phrase 'uber' biker and has had an incredible run at Ironman Western Australia the last three years, having placed second each time. I have no doubt that the top podium step is coming her way there soon.

Michelle Bremer in 6th - Ironman champion galore, she also placed top five in all of her races in 2015, most of which were on the podium. She is as kind and calm off the course as she is strong and consistent on it.

Amanda Stevens in 5th - Another resilient Ironman Champion of all trades, she really never falters. Thirteen years of racing at this level and she still exudes fortitude and strength every time.

Laura Siddall in 4th – Her 4th place performance here is an incredible result especially after her impressive 2nd place at Wanaka just 2 weeks ago. As you can all imagine, it is not an easy feat to do two Iron distance races in that small window of time yet she did it with such grace and stamina. Congrats Sid! I can't wait till that top step of the podium happens for you because I see it on the horizon very soon.

Carrie Lester in 3rd - One of my favorite Aussie's of all time, Carrie really makes things happen out there. She is a multiple Ironman distance champion and also smooth and elegant in her race delivery. She saves all her hustle until the very end, every time.

Lucy Gossage in 2nd – She is a UK Ironman Champion and 10th in Kona this past year. Lucy just rips through the course to the front of the race and embodies true racing excellence.
Congratulations gals! It was a pleasure sharing the day with you all!

It's really important to me personally to make mention of just some of the many folks who make the experience for all of us at Ironman NZ so rewarding!

To the media – Korupt Vision, Delly Carr, Darrell Carey, First off the Bike, Volt TV, Ian Hep and Ironman Live – Thank you for helping to keep people all over the world engaged with our race yesterday.

To the Ironman Crew – Jane, Maria, Helen, Abby, Cameron Harper, Brian and Mike Reilly. **Simply put, you made the day HAPPEN AND FLOW.**

Mike – It was a real privilege to get to share in your 150th IRONMAN VOICE race! We all are fortunate that we got to be a part of that special history with you at the forefront!

To Might River Power and all the volunteers – You all provided the best rolling buffet on the course for all of us racers. We will properly celebrate you and your kindness tomorrow at the Volunteers dinner.

To all the individuals who cheered yesterday – How could you not miss Steve the Croc in his outfit or the fine gentleman banging his pan as we made our first climb out of town! The lovely young gal screaming the word 'GUMPTION' on the run course was music to my ears. If you are here tonight, please know that I was looking for you every loop! In addition, the other lovely Kiwi faithful holding a 'This is your CHI to LOVE Meredith' sign; this all makes my heart sing. Thank you so much.

To SHORTY – Everyone knows who Shorty is in this great town! It is a pleasure being led by SHORTY around the Taupo run course. She puts up with my heavy breathing and inability to chat.

To our NZ family – The Turner Family and The Koenig Family makes it feel like OUR family even though we are very far from home.

To the Prince Motor Lodge for having our same room ready every year. Taupo Thai, Spoon and Paddle and BodyFuel for all the NZ goodness in my belly leading up to the race.

To my inner circle - Kate and Ritch who push, inspire and humble me every day to be a stronger athlete.

To my best friends – Most of you are mothers managing humans every day; you are my heroes.

To my sister, Davo, my parents and my in-laws: I love you all and I value all the support you have given us since the very beginning.

AND to my husband Aaron – I think it's decided that it is imperative that you catch a rainbow trout in the days leading up to the race as that has been our good luck charm over the years. I still pinch myself every day that we get to share in this journey together and explore places like Taupo, NZ.

And lastly to all of you – Having been an age grouper for 9 years myself, I do remember the juggling act it takes to complete and compete in an event like this. You all balance your families, your jobs and LIFE while doing this relentless hobby and passion. Remember to hug your Sherpa, embrace your inner circle, and relish in your achievement.

And so lastly to everyone – KEEP YOUR CHI – surround yourself with people and things that ENRICH your life, do it all with **GUMPTION RADIATING TO FIND YOUR YOU 3.0!!!**

Thanks again so much for having us and we'll see you in December, Taupo!
End

*

Post-Race Recovery and Assessment

Racing is your livelihood, so tasks for a pro triathlete do not end with crossing the finish line. This is the time to critique your performance, heal your body, determine if you are injured, continue marketing your brand, email sponsors, write a blog post, capitalize on momentum generated from the race, and make sure you can put yourself in the best possible position to race again effectively. The seventy-two hours after a race are crucial for your body and brand well-being, so make the time to properly tend to these aspects of your life.

In the hours after a race, my crew is instructed to keep my mind focused on refueling and hydration in order to ensure the next forty-eight hours are pleasant. Migraines and extreme soreness are a direct result of the body not having enough liquids. Not replenishing liquids is tough on your kidneys, which results in an overall unpleasant feeling. You might not be in the frame of mind to proactively do these things, so a little help is necessary. Once I am in a comfortable place, I immediately begin using my Recovery Boots to help with the inevitable leg swelling. The constriction is the same type of recovery that compression socks less effectively try to achieve. It may seem nice to get into a hot tub, but I have found this really makes my body swell. Consequently, I use the combination of Recovery Boots and ice to speed up my recovery. I also take my recovery supplements, outlined in the "Supplements and Vitamins" chapter, to help return to my body some of the precious nutrients it lost on the course. The last step, for me, immediately following a race, is to try to eat something salty. My food of choice is McDonald's French Fries; for some reason, they taste magical!

I have learned that it is tough to sleep for long periods of time after a race. Your body can be confused as to what just happened. I take Melatonin to achieve some sort of a normal slumber, but I still often find myself working on my computer at four in the morning. In the day after a race, I wear my compression socks everywhere, especially if I have to travel long distances or fly on an airplane. The lifting of heavy bags and equipment is difficult, so hopefully your support team will still be around to aid with this; it is tough to travel light in triathlon. You also should be mindful of your body's weakened state and susceptibility to germs. Take precautions to always wash your hands and use Vitamin C or other preventive supplements to combat this. Once I am home, the concentration on hydration and nutrition is still paramount to preparing for training and my next race. Take the time to heal.

The body is resilient, but you have just pushed it to its limits, especially in a full triathlon. A good portion of your major muscles have been broken down, meaning they are ripped and torn and in repair mode. Lactic acid is coursing through the body, adrenaline levels have spiked, and your bodily fluids are all out of whack; this is what racing between two and sixteen hours will do to you. One major effect is how your body swells one to three days after the event; the biggest change occurs after an Ironman. It always amazes me how distorted I look because of the immense swelling; I look like the "Stay Puft Marshmallow Man" from the *Ghostbusters* movies! Do not be alarmed when your body is massively uncomfortable days after the race because it is just its way of recovery. Do not be freaked out by these post-race changes. You should be back to "normal" in five days if you practice proper recovery.

The next priority is to measure the health of your business. Always think of your racing as a business, and after any announcement, product push, or change of policy, a good business takes a step back and assesses the pros and cons of the action. They determine what went according to plan and how they can improve based on how things unfolded. They look internally to figure out the problems, but are not afraid to reach out externally to consultants to analyze the results as well. Talk with your coach about what was successful and what needs work. Do not be afraid to reach out to your doctor if you have lingering ailments or get physical therapy to aid in your recovery. You have to take care of your body just as CEOs take care of their companies; it is how you make a living. If everything goes according to plan, after four days of recovery and recovery workouts you should be able to start again on your regular training regimen. In some respects, I look at racing as a long workout. You will be back to your normal routine as soon as your body recuperates; it is resilient.

The aftermath of triathlon is different from what an athlete in another sport might endure. After a race, questions about your body can arise, and they have to be resolved. I have included below an interaction I had a few years ago with my friend who is a doctor. At the time, I was having trouble with hydration during races and my urine was a grotesque shade of purple. I took the steps to find answers to my post-race problems; the key was to try to do something about it. With my doctor's help and diligent research on my own, I have figured out what my body needs to perform well and end up healthy after a race. The plan I developed works for me—as long as I stick to it! The email below, though, shows how bad a shape I was in *before* I took action.

Excerpt from email to doctor friend:
Interesting enough, I peed more EARLY—three times on the bike. I could NOT pee on the run—did not have to…argh.

My pee—AS ALWAYS after a race—is purple. NO JOKE. PURPLE. It's embarrassing when getting post-race drug tested.

Very very ill post races. ALWAYS. I typically cross the line and have six really big pukes and then my stomach is better. In Wisconsin, I did not get an IV (I did in Canada) because family there, and I did not want them to wait like they did at Canada. All I wanted to do was lay down, get cold water poured over head and puke :) I got to the hotel, had the pukes, and laid in fetal per usual for two hours. Then I could get upright for a bit to chat with all, since they were all so kindly there!!

As for the cramps being worse than menstruating, I get my periods VERY badly—only for about two days but there is a one-day period where it is inhuman how I feel. I kid you not that I plan my race schedule around my period, but sometimes it doesn't work out as such!
Response:
You go to places mortals do not go. You already know this though, and more likely this is why you have been so successful. I believe you are slightly under fueling (+\-), but for sure are WAY low on volume.

I'm a bit nervous about the purple urine, it may be a combo of the energy drinks etc…but more likely some heme/myoglobin pigment, from muscle breakdown and/or blood in the urine. Your kidney function is fine per testing, but I think your symptoms sound an awful lot like heat stress, bordering on Rhabdomyolysis. We need to keep this from happening again!!!

Your post race sounds nightmarish (to me anyway). I think you definitely need more fluid volume during the race. The test you sent suggested at least 750 cc/hour on the bike, you likely need 750–1000 on the run when it's hot. Trick is not sloshing. I think most important is finding a carbo drink with some sodium you can stomach. Blocks are great too—simple rice syrup—but they demand their own water supply to prevent high density sugar globs (wow medical term) laying in your gut, sucking water out of the cells which line the intestine—thereby making you even more dehydrated. Mortals slow down to allow a balance of perfusion to the gut (away from the muscles) to allow absorption. I know slowing isn't an option, so you need essentially a 4 x 8 oz bottle fuel belt per half that you will drink every bit of, in addition to water at the aid stations. What to put in it???? That's really a tough one. Gatorade endurance (G2 now) might work as well as anything else and the folks at Ball State helped with making the mix.

Likewise the gels—great with enough water. The diarrhea is from all the concentrated sugar as well. And you might have a bit of intolerance to one or more of the nutritional products. Lactose???? Avoid any protein; it's usually casein or whey (milk). The GI fluid loss is a problem!!! You are dry already! Given your menstrual history, I think it's a remarkable feat that you can compete during the peak days. WOW!

*

In conclusion, triathlon is not like basketball where you can go out the next day and either build on the momentum from the prior day or try to improve your game immediately. There is a lull between races where there is a lot of time to analyze and dissect your performance; be careful not to overanalyze but make sure you are always moving forward instead of looking over your shoulder. Look for answers to your questions about your racing, implement new concepts in training, and be ready to improve on your next race.

ADVERSITY AND BIKE CRASH

Setbacks are a part of the sport of triathlon. These setbacks can be small or major, depending on the nature of the setback and the amount of time and effort you have dedicated to the sport. Most pro triathletes, including Craig Alexander and Chrissie Wellington, have endured some kind of traumatic injury that has completely derailed their training and, in turn, their confidence. Injuries and other unavoidable complications happen, so be ready to work through them. While this sounds harsh, it is part and parcel of the sport we strive to conquer. Nagging injuries will naturally come with the wear and tear of training and racing over the course of a season. No matter the game face your competition displays before the race, rest assured there is some annoying, lingering injury in the back of their minds that takes their focus, if only a tiny bit, off of the task at hand.

In her book *A Life Without Limits: A World Champion's Journey*, Chrissie Wellington routinely talks about "niggles," which are the everyday afflictions that triathletes face. The lesson I took away from her journey was she rarely went into a race one hundred percent, meaning there was always something, whether a broken wrist, road rash, or tight hamstrings, that impeded her on race day. The reality is *every athlete, every race* is confronted with some health issue; it is how you handle it that counts. It may comfort you to know everyone is worried about something. Some issues are big and some small; it doesn't matter because they are there. We all fight through physical burdens, and that is what makes us triathletes.

A common understanding in our sport is that if you have never been in a bike crash, you are just *waiting* to be in one. Because of the amount of time triathletes are on their bikes, the odds are against us that we will escape some kind of altercation. As I was writing this book, I added yet another calamity to my already growing list of bodily injuries. I was in a horrific bike crash that severely altered what was a dream season for me.

Since I do most of my bike training indoors, I have been dodging my fate effectively for over ten years. However, the triathlon gods finally caught up to me, and I experienced my first major bike crash going forty miles per hour down a steep incline on a hilly road outside of Los Angeles. The rider in front of me lost control of his bike and took a nasty spill, and I had to either try to jump over him, running the risk of crashing into his limp body, or skid off to the right on the solid pavement. I chose the latter, smacking my head with enough force to shatter my Rudy Project helmet, and landing hard on my right side, which took the brunt of the collision with the pavement. The helmet saved my brain from debilitating injuries.

The force of the blow knocked me out briefly. When I revived, I was disoriented but realized I was in one piece. I checked on the other fallen rider who was in agony but coherent. Realizing the severity of the situation, the other riders in our group immediately called an ambulance and the police. The two of us involved in the crash had clouded judgment; our adrenaline was pumping overtime, numbing the pain, and we were stubbornly refusing medical attention. I wanted to finish the ride and was already thinking about the afternoon swim. The other rider was limping severely but resisted going to the hospital as well. After much convincing by our friends and the medical staff on hand, he reluctantly went in the ambulance, and I grudgingly went into the SAG car, throwing my shattered helmet away, shaken but more concerned with finishing the workouts for the day. As it turns out, the other rider broke his hip and either needed a pin or a hip replacement to fix the problem. Luckily, the doctors pinned his hip, and he is on the road to recovery.

For me, when the adrenaline wore off, I could not move, and my back and right side looked like an asteroid field with pieces of gravel, dried blood and abrasions littering my body. I was happy to be alive, but the reality of the situation was now apparent.

The American Midwest mentality is that pain is to be endured. Seeking help is equated with weakness, and the response is to ignore the pain and get back to training. In general, triathletes follow this Midwest method and avoid taking the smart route to determine what is wrong. Consequently they make the injury worse. I refused to go to the hospital in the heat of the moment because I truly did not feel anything was wrong. I then refused help from friends because I did not want anyone to see me in my weakened condition. I spoke to Aaron, who was on a fly-fishing trip in Colorado, and assured him everything was okay, even though he could tell by my voice the pain was immense. He contacted Hillary Biscay who immediately postponed her plans and forced herself into my hotel room to see me lying like a wounded animal, motionless on the bed in the dark. It hurt to even lie down, thus, rest and sleep were out of the question. She helped dress my wounds, get food, and assess the situation; it was apparent something was not right. I am forever grateful to Hillary for coming to my room and nursing me back to sanity.

I barely slept that night, continually waking up in incredible pain and cutting through Advil like a knife through butter. I spoke with Aaron who continued to urge me to go to the hospital. However, my experience with hospitals is I wait for hours to receive attention from a doctor who recommends taking painkillers and rest. This is not a criticism of hospitals but rather a reflection of my belief that doctors are evaluating the severity of the injury itself, without putting it in context of the needs of a professional athlete. The whole process is intimidating and time consuming. If the injury is not deemed life threatening, I then have to see my doctor at home, who will perform another assessment, write a recommendation to see another specialist, and the process becomes endless. I subconsciously avoid this scenario, which was my trepidation in going to the hospital in the first place. However, the pain soon became too intense, and I gave in and asked a friend to take me to the emergency room at six in the morning.

Sure enough, I filled out the paperwork, took some X-rays and received the assessment that I had torn ligaments in my back. Nothing was broken, and I should rest and would be back to normal in ten days. I opted out of painkillers and asked for Ambien so it could help me sleep through the discomfort. I was relieved it was nothing too serious, but I was miffed the pain was something I could not fight through. People informed me a torn ligament can hurt more than one ripped completely through, yet in the back of my mind, something felt very wrong. I decided to heed the words of the doctor and hope the injury would get better in ten days because, let's face it, I liked the diagnosis of a relatively short ten-day recovery.

I was scheduled to fly back to Columbus, Ohio, to visit my parents and train in the heat for ten days. However, I could not move, let alone lift my two large Saucony bags full of gear. Aaron flew from San Francisco to Los Angeles to help nurse me back to health and carry my gear across the country. I do consider myself very pain tolerant and was still annoyed with the diagnosis that I had torn ligaments; the pain was excruciating. I tried to have a calm demeanor around my parents for ten days, but inside, I knew something was really wrong. I still refused to see a specialist because of my general wariness of hospitals; heck, I do not even have a personal doctor I can go to because I have been lucky enough to avoid serious injury. I usually just fight through any discomfort, as most triathletes tend to do.

I was able to get on the bike trainer but with enormous discomfort. I then tried to run on the treadmill and kept telling myself to fight through the piercing pain; this was just a torn ligament. I then jumped in the pool and floundered like a wounded baitfish. Swimming was out of the question, and I had the uncomfortable realization my favorite therapeutic activity was going to be impossible for three to five weeks, which was devastating to my psyche. I was worried about relinquishing my fitness, falling behind my competition, and losing the racing confidence I had generated in 2012. I flew back to San Francisco in complete disarray because the injury was not healing, and I had no answers. The unknown is very frightening when health is concerned.

My mind was running a mile a minute trying to figure out my situation. We had to cancel a "traincation" (training vacation) to Kona because I still could not swim. The answers were eluding me, so I asked a friend who is a doctor for a prescription to get an MRI to check for back injury. I paid for it myself and did not go through the normal insurance channels because the process would have taken two weeks. I also asked another friend to try to get me in immediately to see a physical therapist (PT) since, once again, this would have been a three-week wait. The PT concluded there was something very wrong with my back. He proceeded to crack it multiple times (for realignment), which was extremely painful yet perversely felt good. He then used a vacuum machine on my back. The reasoning behind this was he said my ribs were misaligned, and I had an enormous amount of scar tissue. There were bruises and lumps all over my body from the machine, but I did feel a lot better.

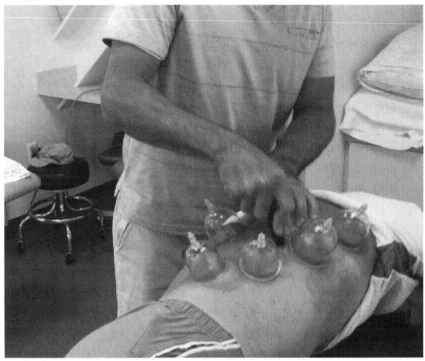

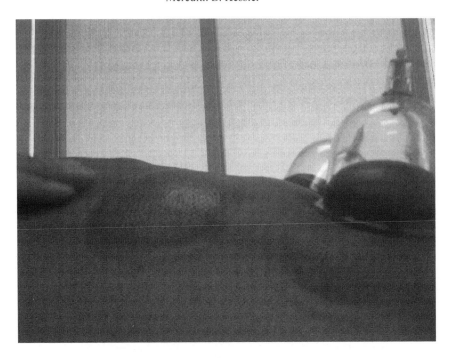

The MRI results came back, and along with the torn ligaments, I discovered I had broken my back! *I sent an email to close family and friends to inform them of the situation:*

Just wanted to again say thank you for all your support and such…really it means so much and all will be fine fine fine of course! Chatted with Dr. Bob this am, and MRI results are back…turns out I have a fracture (AKA break) of the T9 thoracic bone of my spine. It sounds way more dramatic than it is; no important structures are in danger, and just like any fracture, it's a four to six week healing process. Since I'm on week four post crash right now (I know I know—even though I have still been biking and running on it after the initial vampire-state week), I'm now hopefully rounding third base and heading home with this semi-soon—at least in the next couple weeks! *The pros:*
* I FEEL better and in less pain, which obviously is helpful in life (i.e., I'm not cringing when I breath, plus lying down is getting so so so much better:).

* I can continue to bike and run like a crazy person. He said that I have

to let my body be the pain guide, even though I can push through pain, which we know is part of the process...I have been able to push the pavement even in running recently, and my running form is back and the lurking pain subsides each time. His liberal way of thinking is that this actually helps the bone repair through exercise sometimes.

* Kona will happen (maybe even another half end of September depending)...plenty of time to heal and hopefully keep staying in "SHAPE," and once I can swim fully again, I will just work hard to get back in the game in that capacity.

The cons:

* Swimming is still going to take the longest as we know...I tried swimming again today, and it was SO.MUCH.BETTER, but it's still not ready to hit it in there so need to continue to be patient.

* I cannot FALL right now...he said this was of utmost importance to obviously to be careful when running and when biking outside (I have been riding indoors, but he said the six-hour ride on my plan Saturday can happen but obviously to be extra careful, which I will).

* It may be tricky to think that Vegas (Sept. 9) is going to work out...so I can decide week of race...but most likely it may be smart to not race that one as it could put me back for proper Kona prep—we will cross that bridge when we get there!

*

The test results confirmed my feeling that something was not right, and the crash could not have been just torn ligaments. Knowing this answer was what I needed to set my mind at ease, figure out a training plan around the injury, and move forward. I was glad I could toe the line at the Ironman 70.3 World Championships in Las Vegas six weeks after my injury.

I tried to push through the pain, which is always a gray area when it comes to serious injury. The questions that go through an athlete's mind during these situations are numerous and a mental tug of war: How much pain do I endure before risking injury? Will I be perceived as being weak if I break down and see another doctor? What if they discover something is really wrong with my body? How will I compete in my next race? What will my sponsors, family, and friends think?

In reality, I should have seen a specialist immediately when I got to Columbus, no matter how I was feeling. The problem is that athletes have ingrained in them, since grade school, this idea that they must show no weakness—that they must fight through pain. This is no excuse for not seeing a specialist, but it is what happens in ninety percent of these gray-area situations. Although most of us learn how we deal with adversity only after encountering it, I offer my story with the hope you will learn from my situation and confirm the extent of your injuries as soon as you can. I believe I have learned from this experience and will contact a specialist when unusual health issues occur.

What can you learn from my bike crash adversity?

- Find a doctor you can trust before encountering adversity. This will save time and energy when the inevitable traumatic event occurs.

- Secure health insurance. Though it may sound redundant, this is a *must* as a triathlete.

- Do not be surprised when pain hits a few hours after the event. Adrenaline masks the pain and injury immediately following an accident.

- Determine the problem before it gets worse. This is easier said than done because the human brain is wired to push through pain and discomfort.

- Do not be afraid to ask for help. I could not have gotten through my ordeal without help from my family and friends. This includes networking for doctors and specialists, as well as for emotional and physical support.

- Know that you are not alone. Every triathlete has had a physical hardship, and your competitors may be going through one on race day. You are rarely one hundred percent when you toe the line at a race.

- Do not overreact to one bad race, searching for "answers" to a problem after a disappointing finish. Some days you have it, and some days you do not. There is no such thing as a perfect race. If there are a string of bad races, you should then search for answers.

- Know your pain levels, and if something does not feel right, trust your judgment and decide what to do.

- Do not rush back into training before you have gauged the extent of your injury. This can lead to larger problems requiring more time, energy, and mental anguish.
- Do not neglect your normal routine when preparing for an event if you do race after facing adversity. Problems with your nutrition and hydration could arise, or problems in other areas that will affect your race, simply because you were concentrating on the injury and not your whole body.

Adversities come in many forms, from blunt trauma injuries to the behind-the-scenes bodily fatigue. I have a friend who had overwhelming fatigue on race days, which resulted in subpar performances and even an inability to finish races. She searched for months trying to find an answer, speaking to a multitude of specialists with theories but no remedies. Finally, a friend suggested it could be an allergy to something she eats every day or before races. She gave this idea some credence, and tests revealed she had allergies specific to foods she was eating in her daily routine and around races. After changing her eating patterns, she now feels better training and on race day. This improvement came about because of her dedication to defining the problem and doing something about it.

I have used golf as an analogy many times in this manual because it is very similar to triathlon in the dedication, time, effort, luck, and perseverance it takes to succeed. Perfection in both racing and golf never exists, and the earlier you understand this fact, the faster you will be able to reach your goals in either one of these sports. This does not mean there are not those perfect *moments* that keep the triathlete searching for the race when everything comes together. I am a horrible golfer, but there is always one shot per round where everything goes right. It is that singular magical shot where all of my golf lessons and practice rounds come together for one graceful moment. This keeps me coming back, and this is the exact sensation triathletes feel on race day that keeps them wanting more. The moments can be few and far between, but they are so gratifying that triathletes are back the next week in the cycling studio searching for more of them. It wouldn't be triathlon if everyone could do it.

The next time you play a round of golf, poll golfers in the clubhouse afterwards and find out how many people say they played to the best of their abilities. Do the same exercise after a triathlon; ask racers if they performed to their expectations, and ask them their overall impressions of the race. You will find ninety-five percent of the athletes in both categories find fault with their performances, point to ailments or what they did wrong, and are not completely satisfied with the results. The more time and energy you put into the activity, the more critical you will be of your performance. After missing a shot, the casual golfer smiles and continues to the next hole. The golfer who has put years into perfecting his or her game may throw a tantrum, worry endlessly about what went wrong, and potentially squeeze the fun out of his or her day. We have all been in this group at some point in our athletic careers.

The interesting group is the five percent who defy the odds and, in their eyes, had a wonderful race or round. They will remember the day for the rest of their lives. Chris Wright, the writer of the foreword to this manual, still gushes over his race at Vineman. He was not expecting to get into the race, but a spot opened up a week before the event. He had a slight cold and was not prepared, but he drove up from Los Angeles to Sonoma, California, and proceeded to have the race of his life; his equipment, body, and mind were in perfect alignment. This is the reason people race: to be the five percent who experience a kind of nirvana on the course. All of the pain endured, hardships overcome, and time spent is worth it for that one moment— that elusive, synchronous moment that keeps bringing athletes back, time and time again.

In contrast, one of my athletes ran a very good time in an Ironman but was upset because he did not reach his pre-race goal. He threw his medal away in disgust and stormed back to his hotel room. The next morning, he saw an athlete with a medal around her neck. She asked him how his race was, and he described not reaching his goal. Grinning ear to ear, she described her race, ecstatic about being able to finish twenty minutes before the race closed; she had experienced the race of *her* life. My athlete took a step back and realized it was just a race; some dreams were made that day and others remained just out of reach.

Racing is one giant jigsaw puzzle that every competitor has to figure out, or that beautiful race will continue to be elusive. If one piece is missing or misaligned, it throws the whole puzzle off. You have to work hard to find the solution and determine why certain pieces don't fit. Without these answers, you cannot perform at the level to which you strive. Defining the problem and working through it is what makes the sport such a challenge.

Athletes plan all year to have the perfect race. It might be at Kona or a 70.3 they planned to attend months in advance. Whether you are a pro or an amateur, keep in mind there is a real possibility your perfect race will not happen due to the complexity of triathlons. Adversity plays a large role in this sport, and it often throws another wrinkle into the overall plan. I obviously did not want to break my back after having one of the proudest moments in my race career at Vineman 2012 and before two of the most important races of the season. I worked hard to get to a point where I could toe the line at the Vegas 70.3 World Championships, only to be derailed by severe dehydration as a result of not drinking enough in the Vegas heat in the days prior to the race. This, coupled with the fact that I was taking four to six ibuprofen a day for my back, severely hurt my kidneys to the point where, physically, I was out of the race before I even started. I successfully conquered my known adversity, but my focus was diverted from the other aspects of my training, which eventually disrupted my comeback.

Everyone faces hardships. Major—and minor—obstacles are simply a part of the sport, and they have the power to be extremely devastating. The serious triathlete spends countless hours tinkering and tweaking his or her game. If there is an ailment or something is not right, an athlete will continuously search until the problem is discovered and hopefully resolved. Not every race will be ideal. Sometimes things go wrong without a specific reason, but we must keep it in perspective, go back to the drawing board, and race another day.

I began my comeback journey not wanting anyone to know about my accident, but I soon realized everyone has "niggles" to worry about. In triathlon, you compete against yourself, against the course, and—last on the list—against your competitors. Every pro is in the zone, trying to plan for the task at hand, and whoever shows up is who will be raced against. The memory of the race will be gone in a week, and life goes on.

PARTING WORDS

After years of reflection, I have developed a list of things that I have personally learned along this triathlon journey, and how we all struggle to get to the finish line. Hopefully you can take some of these concepts to help you on your triathlon journey and fight to the finish line when times get tough, which they understandably will, over the course of a season.

1. Keep it simple. Less is more. Try your best not to over think things. As long as you have your wetsuit, bike, helmet, race kit, biking shoes, sunscreen, running shoes, sunglasses, and race nutrition, you are good to go! Be relaxed.

2. There will be high and low moments during the day. The highs will be HIGH and the lows will be LOW. Just remember that in those low moments, you will prevail. You will find gumption and rise above.

3. Problem solve: Think about everything you have done to get to that moment. This will help inspire you to keep going and keep strong. You have to keep thinking pain is temporary and you will not remember how you feel IN THAT MOMENT when you cross the finish line.

4. Visualize: Keep replaying yourself crossing the finish line at your goal time or just in general. Replay, replay, replay, and then when you are IN the moment that you have been visualizing, it will be beyond worth it.

5. Nutrition! Nutrition! Nutrition! Rolling buffet. Most of the time if you are "losing it," it is due to calories, so be diligent with your calories. Hydration, nutrition, hydration, nutrition.

6. IT WILL SETTLE. I say these words to myself over and over again in a race. IT WILL SETTLE. Whatever I may feel during a period of time, it will settle, and I will rise above any issues that may arise.

7. SWIM: Pretend the first five hundred yards is a FAST effort. You'll find that if you go a little bit faster from the get-go, you will locate your "pack" and be able to find your groove.

8. BIKE/RUN: Try to go for some negative split action for both. Focus on calories and settling in on the first several miles of each, and then find your groove and gun it the second half.

9. Most importantly HAVE FUN AND KCCO (Keep calm, carry on!) all day long. The day is all yours! The hard work is done, and the race is simply a celebration of it all! Believe in yourself and all that you have done (and the people who helped you along the way). Encourage others and enjoy the finish!

10. MANAGE THE MINDSET. I genuinely believe that training and racing in our sport IS A MINDSET. A very marquee and important MINDSET. The slightest SHIFT in our mindset can make or break so many things in triathlon and in life. We have to train this mindset to DELIVER in practice and on race day. It's a HARD and TEDIOUS job to do yet when it is also practiced like we do in the swim, bike, and run, it can get better overtime to be in the RIGHT, POSITIVE, THRIVING mindset 99.9% of the time. Sure, we are allowed to FEEL and it's ok to be 'off' in the mindset at times (just like in training) yet the more powerful our mindset is, the stronger we are as humans.

11. Preparation breeds confidence. This includes not only preparing the BODY for what we put it through yet also preparing the mind. I like to dive into the art of *Getting Comfortable Being Uncomfortable* (GCBU). Within specific (but certainly not all) workouts/racing/mindsets, it is these raw, tender, gentle moments of discomfort where the magic actually happens.

12. We compete against others at the end of the day yet that isn't what drives us to compete in the first place. We are inspired to compete TOGETHER in order to see, individually, where WE are in sport. I view racing as a constant evolution of progression, learning, fine-tuning and recalibrating. Racing is filled with the most intense moments; ones that also bring us the most extreme and raw possibility. These moments enable us to craft meaning in what we have been doing with effort, stamina, gumption, fortitude and of course FAILURE. If we don't fail, if we don't lose, what will drive us to be better?

NEVER LET SUCCESS GET TO YOUR HEAD, OR FAILURES GET TO YOUR HEART. This mindset is how we all THRIVE.

COPYRIGHT & DISCLAIMER NOTICES

Meredith Kessler, Inc.
lifeoftriathlete@gmail.com
www.meredithkessler.com
www.lifeoftriathlete.com

The book is available at www.lifeoftriathlete.com and
www.meredithkessler.com and will be available in most major
electronic media outlets

Created in the United States of America

Meredith and Aaron's Disclaimer

This book was written after years of personal experience in triathlon,
and the concepts discussed have worked for Meredith in that sport.
You should consult a doctor, tax attorney, and triathlon coach before
following Meredith's personal plan. Please give thoughtful deliberation
to all the areas of the triathlon experience before starting and executing
your triathlon journey.

You have permission to print the e-book in its entirety for your
personal use as a hard copy guide. We ask that you not reproduce our
e-book for resale or distribution. It is for Personal Use Only, as the
proceeds allow Meredith to continue her dream of being a pro
triathlete.

We did not get paid to promote anyone in this book.

Publisher's Disclaimer

The material in this book is for informational purposes only. As each
individual situation is unique, use proper discretion in consultation with
a health care practitioner, doctor, tax attorney, or triathlon coach
before undertaking the techniques described in this book. The author
and publisher expressly disclaim responsibility for any adverse effects
that may result from the use or application of the information

contained in this book.

License Notes

ABOUT THE AUTHORS

Meredith B. Kessler is a pro triathlete, cycling instructor, triathlete coach, and multiple Ironman champion. She travels the world racing competitively, while balancing family, friends, and training. She is stepping into the literary world with her first manuals, *Life of a Triathlete: Race Preparation and Life of a Triathlete: Business*. She resides in Marin, California with her husband, Aaron. Visit Meredith online at www.meredithkessler.com, or follow her on Twitter (@mbkessler) and Facebook, to find out more about her, as well as her sponsors, blog, and past and future race schedule.

Aaron Kessler is an entrepreneur and outdoorsman. His current projects include laying the foundation for the Life of a Triathlete movement, consulting for Continental Message Solution, and developing ways to help aspiring triathletes reach their athletic and business goals. He graduated from Harvard University where he played four years of varsity baseball, and he resides in Marin, California. Follow him on Twitter at @lifetriathlete and @kessler32.

Made in the USA
San Bernardino, CA
09 September 2016